'Dearest Augustus and I':
The Journal of Jane Pugin

Edited & with an introduction by
Caroline Stanford

'Dearest Augustus and I':
The Journal of Jane Pugin

Edited & with an introduction by
Caroline Stanford

Spire Books Ltd
in association with
The Landmark Trust

Published by
Spire Books Ltd
PO Box 2336
Reading RG4 5WJ
www.spirebooks.com

in association with
The Landmark Trust
Shottesbrooke
Maidenhead SL6 3SW
www.landmarktrust.co.uk

CIP data:
A catalogue record for this book is available
from the British Library
ISBN 0-9543615-8-X

Designed and produced by John Elliott
Text set in Adobe Bembo

Printed by Alden Group Ltd
Osney Mead
Oxford OX2 0EF

Cover photograph:
Jane Pugin by G. A. Freezor, 1859
(*Palace of Westminster Collection*)

Back:
Card announcing Jane and Pugin's marriage in 1848 (*reproduced in Benjamin Ferrey*, Recollections of A. W. N. Pugin and his Father Augustus Pugin, *1861*).

For Julian, my husband

Contents

ACKNOWLEDGEMENTS

◆ ◆ ◆

In any field of scholarship, the newcomer must clamber
gratefully onto the shoulders of giants who have gone
before. This has been especially so in the case of
Augustus Pugin and his house in Ramsgate. Pugin
scholarship is a relatively recent discipline but the highest
standards have been set from the outset. Alexandra
Wedgwood's scholarly, annotated catalogues quickly
become the bibles of anyone trying to make sense of the
huge amount of evidence Pugin left of his life and I am
particularly grateful to Lady Wedgwood for reading this
volume at proof stage and for characteristically helpful
suggestions.

Despite large deposits of Pugin materials in public
research libraries, much still remains in private collections
and I am extremely grateful for the generous permission to
publish the journal itself (a facsimile is on deposit at the
House of Lords Record Office) and various illustrations by

private owners. Thanks too to the staff at the House of Lords Record Office, the Parliamentary Estates Directorate, the V & A Picture Library and the English Heritage Photo Library.

Finally, thanks are due to Spire Books Ltd. for agreeing to publish this volume in association with the Landmark Trust.

Caroline Stanford
November 2003

FOREWORD

♦ ♦ ♦

Jane Pugin had a long and eventful life: the happiness of her marriage in August 1848, life at The Grange, Ramsgate, and the birth of her two children, and then the sadness and drama of her husband's final illness and death in September 1852, are here recorded in her own words.

The immediate emotional and financial difficulties and responsibilities that she faced as a young widow are hinted at, and must have been very hard to bear. Not much detail is known of the period she and the family spent in Birmingham, but their return to The Grange in 1861 was triumphant. By this time Edward Pugin, his father's eldest son, was becoming a successful architect and the 1860s must have been good times for the family. Jane was clearly a well-liked step-mother, with her relationship to Edward, who was some nine years younger, being particularly close. Edward, however, in spite of his undoubted abilities, was impetuous and argumentative. In 1872, the year in which he made a number of important alterations to The Grange, his involvement with the development of the immense and luxurious Granville Hotel on the East Cliff at Ramsgate ended in his bankruptcy. This must have been a great blow to the whole family and it was followed in June 1875 by his death. Jane would again have experienced considerable emotional and financial difficulties, and perhaps this explains the two verses dated Ramsgate 1876, which she inscribed at the end of her journal, and which ask for Freedom and Health. She clearly had the character and resilience to overcome her problems; always loyal to her husband's memory, she lived on at The Grange with her stepson, Cuthbert, before moving to St Edward's Presbytery, the little house that Pugin built for the priest between The Grange and the church. There she remained – one last sadness must have been a fire in the roof of The Grange in 1904 – a formidable grandmother to the extended family until her death in 1909.

Jane's determination ensured The Grange's survival in the nineteenth century; the twentieth century brought difficult times for the house before it was rescued in the 1990s by the Landmark Trust who recognised its importance. It is indeed appropriate that Caroline Stanford, the historian of the Landmark Trust, has preserved the memory of this remarkable woman with this poignant book, the royalties of which are going to the restoration of The Grange. I have pleasure in recommending it.

Alexandra Wedgwood
Patron of the Pugin Society
November 2003

My journal from the year
I was married.

Augt. 10th I was married at
St George's Church by Fr Doyle
the head chaplain there were present My Husband, Uncle Knile
& Aunt, Annie Edward & Agnes
Angie. Mr Herbert B.A. Rev —
J. Telford (to whom I made my general confession) Talbot. Cotter
after Mass at which we received
the most Holy Communion we
returned to Welworth House
at 1/2 past 9 and breakfasted
we left there for the railway
at 1/2 past 11 and arrived
at Ramsgate at 1/2 past 3 o'c
the flag was hoisted for the first
time! Cuthbert. Catherine and
Mary, with Sarah & Mary the
servants were ready to receive

INTRODUCTION

Caroline Stanford

♦ ♦ ♦

*I have got a first-rate Gothic woman at last, who perfectly
understands and delights in spires, chancels, screens, stained
glass, brasses, vestments etc.*[1]

So wrote Augustus Pugin to his client and friend, the
Rev. James John Hornby, on the occasion of his
marriage to Jane Knill. Pugin had been a widower
since the death of his second wife, Louisa Burton, in 1844
and the single state did not suit him. He had first married
Anne Garnet in 1831 when he was only nineteen years old
and she only seventeen. A daughter, named after her
mother, was born the next year but, tragically, Anne died
after only a year's marriage. Pugin then married Louisa
Burton in 1833 and she bore him five more children:
Edward (1834-75), Agnes (1836-95), Cuthbert (1840-
1928), Katherine (1841-1927) and Mary (1843-1921).
Pugin was married to Louisa for the longest of his three

wives, but only Jane, his last wife, left a journal behind to record her married life and it is therefore her voice that we hear most clearly today.

Augustus Welby Northmore Pugin (1812-52) was one of the most influential and prolific architects and designers of the nineteenth century. In his brief, forty-year life span Pugin threw his whole being into realising in architecture and the decorative arts his belief that Gothic was the only style fit for a Christian society. He looked back wistfully and sometimes whimsically to mediaeval society, which he considered far superior to the increasingly mechanised and secular one he saw around him. A devout convert to English Roman Catholicism, Pugin reverently and fervently espoused and promoted the Catholic liturgy in the many churches he built. To these may be added schools, convents, monasteries and houses – quite apart from designing the interiors for the Houses of Parliament. Passionate, intense, naïve, impatient, combative and funny, Pugin worked ceaselessly as he sought to recreate in his own life and works the Gothic life which he idealised. He had a loyal team of colleagues, whose craftsmen and builders translated his countless designs into reality. He was also a perfectionist, seeing himself as 'the scholar and representative of those Glorious Catholic architects who lived in antient days and to whom the merit of all our present performances are in justice to be referred … I seek *antiquity* and not *novelty*. I strive to *revive not invent* and when I have done my best and when compared with the puny and meagre abortions of the day I have produced a sturdy effect yet how terribly do my best efforts sink when tested by the scale of antient excellence.'[2] Such a man cannot have been easy to live with, yet he was clearly at ease with and attractive to women.

Once left a widower with six children at Louisa's death, Pugin had wasted little time seeking another wife. Mary

Fig. 1
A. W. N. Pugin, by J.R. Herbert, 1845
(*Palace of Westminster Collection*)

Amherst, daughter of one of his patrons, had declined his proposal in the months after he became a widower to his deep disappointment. A further engagement fell by the wayside as Pugin's friends convinced him that the lady was not for him.[3] The children, meanwhile, were being faithfully cared for by a Miss Greaves, a family friend who stayed at The Grange from autumn 1844 to spring 1846. She seems to have had hopes of her own of becoming the third Mrs Pugin but it was not to be.[4]

In 1846 Pugin began an intense courtship with Helen Lumsden which lasted till 1848 and his letters to her give us a vivid picture of the state of mind of this brilliant, driven architect and designer when left without a soulmate. He wrote that before he found her 'I was rapidly falling into a misanthropic state of mind … till very lately my hair came off in combfulls but from the time of your affection nothing of this kind has occurred to me.'[5] He expressed his need succinctly: 'a really affectionate faithful woman is worth the whole world … there is no trial a man cannot support when so blessed'[6] and was clearly wretched without a helpmate. 'To live without my beloved is utter misery', he wrote. 'I feel like a mariner at sea without a compass. My house is sad & lonely, night after night I have sat alone in my library too unhappy to study. I often return from a long journey, the children retired to rest, no one to greet me. I only see a servant & my heart sinks within me.'[7]

Helen Lumsden, a Protestant from Edinburgh, agreed to marry Pugin on 25th January 1848 and also to join him in the Catholic faith. The wedding dress, designed by Pugin and made by his decorator J. G. Crace, was finished by 30th March when Pugin instructed that it be sent by 'quick train', but it was already too late. At the last minute, Helen broke off the engagement, giving way, it seems, to her relations' resistance to her joining the Catholic Church.

Being afraid that friends would think he had behaved in an underhand manner, Pugin was moved to publish a pamphlet, called *A Statement of Facts*. 'As soon as my union with Miss L— had been definitely arranged,' he wrote, 'I immediately proceeded to make the necessary arrangements by altering and completing my residence, making new furniture, plate etc., and providing dresses, jewellery, etc.'[8] Such was Pugin's disappointment that he even published private letters between himself and his fiancée, as much it seems in an attempt to express his own sense of betrayal as to defuse any whisper of impropriety that might surround a broken engagement.

Two months later, Pugin met Jane Knill and it is a sign both of the ease with which he could transfer his affections and of his need for a wife and a mother for his children that six weeks later they were married. Jane was the niece and adopted daughter of John Knill (her father had died when she was eight). Knill was a benefactor of St George's in Southwark (later the first Catholic cathedral in England for over 300 years) and had chaired the committee that raised funds for the grand opening ceremony. The church was built to Pugin's design (although his first ambitions for it were limited by available funds) and Knill must have met Pugin during this process. It therefore seems highly probable that it was Knill who first introduced Pugin to Jane.

The Knills were an old family from Herefordshire. Jane was born on 21st June 1825 and her baptism is recorded in the parish registers of Tedstone Delamere, a daughter to Thomas Knill, farmer and Elizabeth Knill of Tipton Hall.[9] Tedstone Delamere is a village near Bromyard, about 20 miles east of Knill Court, the mediaeval seat of the Herefordshire Knills (now a ruin). Jane's father died in 1833 and her mother and siblings were still to be found in

Fig. 2
Jane Pugin, by G. A. Freezor, 1859. Painted seven years after Pugin's death,
Jane is wearing jewellery designed by Pugin, some originally intended for
Helen Lumsden but which he gave to Jane at their marriage.
(*Palace of Westminster Collection*)

Fig. 3
Card announcing Jane and Pugin's marriage in 1848,
showing the conjoined arms of both families
(*reproduced in Benjamin Ferrey,* Recollections of
A. W N. Pugin and his Father Augustus Pugin, 1861).

Whitbourne, nearby, in the late 1830s. By 1841, her uncle John Knill was in possession of Tipton Hall, which had 238 acres and was managed by three tenant farmers. John Knill himself was based in London, owner of a flourishing firm of wharfingers just east of London Bridge. He had a daughter of the same age as Jane and may have informally adopted Jane after her father's death and brought her to live in his London home, Walworth House. Alternatively, she may have come to London to broaden her horizons rather later.

Jane was baptised an Anglican - before the Act for the Relief of Catholics in 1829 (popularly known as Catholic Emancipation), it required a stern faith indeed to adopt Catholicism publicly. Pugin was characteristically early in his conversion, which occurred in 1835 and his wife Louisa joined him in 1839. In 1842, John Knill converted to Catholicism, together with his immediate family. Critically for her future relationship with Pugin, it seems likely that Jane joined them in their conversion. This was a brave move, some years before the wave of prominent conversions which followed that by John Henry Newman in 1845. As far as Pugin was concerned, Jane therefore had everything: not just youth and beauty but a mediaeval pedigree and sound Catholic beliefs. Unlike Helen Lumsden, she was supported and encouraged in her faith by her family.

By the time Jane met Pugin, both John and his son Stuart were active in the community around St George's in Southwark. They became important benefactors to the church, commissioning, for example, a pyx from Pugin.[10] Stuart and Pugin were also firm friends and family connections were to persist: after John's death in 1854, Stuart commissioned a chantry for the family at St George's from Pugin's eldest son Edward.

Jane was almost twenty-three when she met Pugin (he was thirty-six). The first entry in Pugin's diary that may refer to her is on 5th June 1848. He had returned to his home, The Grange in Ramsgate, on 3rd June. On 5th June he notes 'Mrs. Knill and dined here.' (Pugin's diary is rarely more than the briefest jottings of where he had spent the day.) His next mention of Jane, some six weeks later on 22nd July, records: 'Dearest Jane affianced to me.'[11] As usual, Pugin had been away during the weeks in between, on multiple trips to Birmingham, Liverpool, Dublin, Rugby and Alton to oversee projects, so it must indeed have been a whirlwind romance.

Two days after their engagement, he wrote to Jane from Ramsgate:

> My Dearest Jane
> I had almost hoped for a few lines from you this morning but I suppose you froze the ink & could not get on. I have been incessantly occupied all day, what between drawing and clearing out my cabinets &c. for you, I have not had a moment. You will find a capital wardrobe to stow away all your things. Agnes [aged 12] is delighted at your coming - & so is Edward [aged 14]. The house has been miserably dead for them for want of a head & they have seen their father always in distress of mind & now all will be changed & they will be doubly happy. When I told Agnes she said she knew it, Miss Headley told her – so it cannot be any secret here.[12]

Jane and Pugin were married on 10th August 1848 at St George's, the first wedding to be held in the church. Both gave Walworth House as their place of residence on their marriage certificate, a device that gave Pugin residency within the parish for registration for the sacrament. The marriage was loyally attended by the priests at St George's. Their leader Dr Doyle wrote to express his regret that none of the clergy from St George's could attend the opening of

Fig. 4

A True Prospect of Saint Augustine's Church now Erecting at Ramsgate in the Isle of Thanet, watercolour exhibited at the Royal Exhibition in 1849. The Grange is the house to the left. The painting represents Pugin's vision of his ideal family home nestling against a religious settlement, just as it might have done in the Middle Ages (the sea lies out of the view at the bottom of the garden). The seated figure on the iron seat in the garden might well be Jane; three young children play on the lawn. This happy family scene is in contrast to the spiritual work of the monks across the garden wall as they attend a burial. In fact the painting is not quite accurate in its minor detail of The Grange, showing rather how Pugin wished he had built it (for example, the break in the elevation facing the garden). Pugin lived to see the consecration of the church in 1851. After his early death, his son Edward was to complete the monastic buildings, including the church, which never acquired its spire.

(Private Collection)

Fig. 5
The Grange in 2003, before restoration by the Landmark Trust.
(*The Landmark Trust*)

a new church at Salford on 9th August 1848, adding as their excuse that:

> without publishing the circumstances which kept them all at home, one may just hint at a very interesting celebration that took place in the chapel of our Blessed Lady on St. Laurence's Day, 10 August. It was the first of its kind in St. George's, and the very building itself seemed to know the principal parties engaged therein. We all regretted the stern necessity which bound us hand and foot at home, yet one is compelled at times to take things for better or worse.[13]

Other friends and patrons were unreserved in their delight and relief that Pugin had found another partner. Lord Shrewsbury, one of Pugin's most loyal and generous patrons, wrote in reply to the card announcing the marriage 'I can assure you that nothing has given me more pleasure for a long time past than the announcement of your sudden and happy marriage. Providence I am sure has now rewarded you for all your past sufferings and given you a happy home for the rest of your days.'[14]

Despite the whirlwind romance, there can be little doubt of the strength of affection between them. Jane, who can hardly not have been aware of Pugin's failed engagement with Helen, wore the jewellery designed for her predecessor. Pugin believed strongly in the symbolism of jewellery. He had written to Helen, 'Everybody should have a good set of jewels for great feasts and solemnity, it is an antient & laudable custom. I abhor extravagance but all that is suitable to Rank & function should be carefully kept up.'[15] Fortunately, the only changes required for Jane to inherit the lovely parure he had designed for Helen were new monograms and armorials on the casket and a re-cut seal. The jewellery has become firmly associated with Jane through Freezor's portrait (see Fig. 2). The set also acquired its own fame by being displayed in Pugin's Mediaeval Court at the Great Exhibition in 1851, where it was admired by Queen Victoria herself who 'specially requested to see them, before inspecting the other objects in the exhibition'.[16] From later photographs, it seems Jane wore the jewellery on more than just special occasions.[17]

Jane's journal begins with the day of her wedding and covers the four years of the marriage until Pugin's early death, aged only forty, in 1852. The early part of her writing is clearly being done from memory and at a later date. Her account of her husband's final months has a greater sense of immediacy. She wrote in a small pocket book, measuring some 10 cm by 16 cm. It cannot have been easy for the 23-year-old, arriving to be the stepmother of six children ranging in age from Pugin's eldest daughter by his first marriage, Anne, who was sixteen, to his youngest child by Louisa, Mary, who was only five in 1848. Jane was to have two children of her own with Pugin, Margaret (born 1849) and Edmund (later known as Peter Paul, born in 1851). Yet she seems to have won the hearts of all the children, who were 'handsome like their parents, and brown and hardy from blowing about in gales,'[18] and was to keep the family together until her own death, some 57 years after her husband, in 1909. John Hardman Powell, the nephew of Pugin's metalwork and stained glass supplier John Hardman of Birmingham, came to live with Pugin in Ramsgate in 1844 in the dark days after Louisa's death. He wrote of Jane:

A step-Mother's position is always a difficult one, the more so when she has children of her own, but she won the praise of all. Mrs. Pugin says that when she heard him [Pugin] storming outside at some stupid workmen, he would come in with a smile on his face and answered her surprise by 'I'm not such a brute as to be angry with you.'[19]

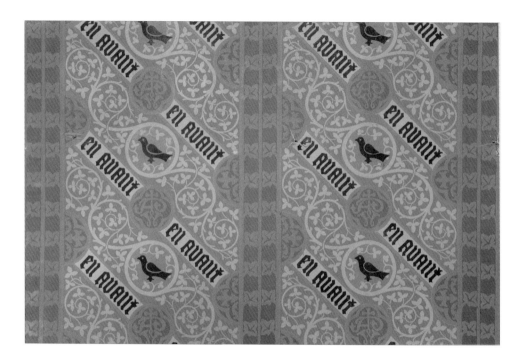

Fig. 6
The wallpaper Pugin designed for The Grange and used in different colourways throughout the house. It features his motto, *En Avant* and family emblem, the black martlet. This version was found beneath panelling in a bedroom at The Grange.
(*John Miller*)

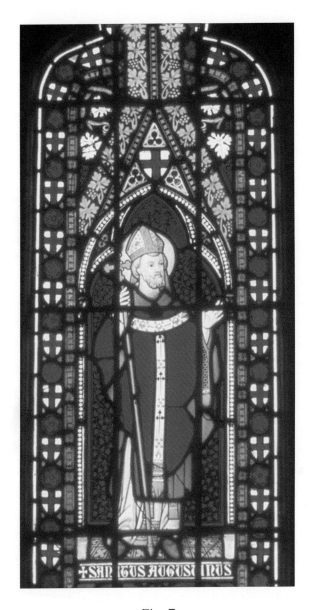

Fig. 7
Detail from a stained glass window in Pugin's
private chapel at The Grange, thought to be
designed by William Wailes *c*.1844. St
Augustine was Pugin's favourite saint.
(*The Landmark Trust*)

Jane also became mistress of The Grange, the house designed by Pugin and constructed by his builder, George Myers, first for his life with Louisa Burton and then significantly refurbished for the putative arrival of Helen Lumsden, to whom he had written, 'I am full of work at the house improving everything before you come so that we shall have nothing to do but enjoy the place afterwards. I am making great alterations ... altering the nursery, panelling the Dining [or drawing?] room altering shields &c & in fact fitting out in every department.'[20] Here too there must have been ghosts for his new bride to exorcise but, as the journal reveals, they shared happy times in the house.

Pugin had spent happy childhood holidays in Ramsgate with a favourite aunt, Selina Welby. Her legacy in 1834 helped him to build his first house, St Marie's Grange near Salisbury, and it was to Ramsgate that Pugin decided to return with his second wife Louisa and their growing family in 1843. In 1841 he bought a plot of land on the West Cliff, then an area of open fields (see Figs 4 & 5) and proceeded to plan his ideal family home, to be erected in the Gothic style and nestling under the walls of a church. According to Hardman Powell, to 'build a Church out of his own earnings' was the one ambition of Pugin's life.[21] At that stage, he envisaged the house as a happy family home with Louisa and the six children. It is she who is shown kneeling with Anne and two other children in the attitude of a mediaeval donor beneath St Gregory in the south light of the two-light east window above the altar in the private chapel at The Grange. Pugin kneels facing her in the north light, beneath St Augustine, his patron saint (see Figs 7 & 8). The fact that St Augustine had landed in Britain near Ramsgate at Ebbsfleet in 597 and the area's strong associations with early Christianity only added to Ramsgate's appeal for Pugin.

The Grange itself is a seminal building, although it is perhaps hard at first glance to appreciate the full importance of the shift in architectural style it represented because so much of subsequent English domestic architecture came to reflect it. At the time, Pugin was radical in his departure from the external symmetry of Classical architecture, which he abhorred as 'pagan'. He built his home around the internal function of its rooms, intimate in scale and in its external architectural expression. It was a family house but also one in which Pugin was inspired to some of his finest work, despite the presence of all the children. In his library there he did many of the designs for the fitting out of the House of Lords; at times it was a showcase for his furnishing designs for clients.[22] The eyewitness accounts, Pugin's watercolours and archaeological evidence make clear that the interiors were intensely colourful and dominated throughout by the family motto, 'En Avant', and the little black martlet from the Pugin family arms (see Figs 6 & 9). It was also a devoutly Christian house and, as well as the private chapel, there was a large statue of the Virgin and Child displayed prominently in the entrance hall. Such was the family home of which Jane became mistress.

Jane and Pugin's courtship was so brief that there are few traces of their relationship before their marriage. Afterwards they corresponded copiously, the opportunity provided by Pugin's frequent absences from home. His letters to her are full of his work and instructions as well as affection; they are clearly devoted to each other and there is a gently teasing tone, especially in Jane's letters to Pugin:

> I was sorry dearest that you sent back your great coat with Father Costogan [sic] as I very much fear you will find it cold in London especially in the evening. I thought you were a <u>prudent</u> <u>man</u>. I suppose you march about in your

Fig. 8

Detail from a stained glass window in the private chapel at The Grange
depicting Pugin at prayer, in the attitude characteristic of a mediaeval
donor and perhaps intended to represent Pugin in more mature years
than he was to attain. Design attributed to William Wailes, *c*.1844.
(*The Landmark Trust*)

Fig. 9

Minton tiles in the floor of the
entrance hall at The Grange.
These carry alternately the Pugin
family arms with the black martlet and Pugin's monogram, AWP.
(*The Landmark Trust*)

mackintosh, you will therefore not look <u>over</u> <u>bewitching</u>. You have therefore my permission to take your walk in Oxford Street any time you like. I am sure it is very kind of me to allow you. – ...I seem to love you dearest more and more, I trust God will give us <u>many</u> <u>many</u> <u>years</u> <u>together</u>. I can never thank him sufficiently for giving me such a Husband.[23]

Pugin missed Jane dreadfully when he travelled. 'I feel constantly anxious about you,' he wrote from Garendon in October 1848:

You are my second existence ... it is miserable travelling alone. There is such a contrast to the delightful journey we had together [their honeymoon] & I am obliged to go through Ely where we were together.[24]

Life on the road was not easy and Pugin invariably set himself a punishing itinerary. The following letter to Jane from Dublin, written in May 1849, is typical:

I have had very little rest since I started & last night there was so much row in the hotel I could not sleep. How I long for my snug birth [*sic*] by the side of my own. I think of you constantly & wish you were with me – but you could not stand the fatigue.[25]

It was Pugin's custom to travel on the Continent every summer, partly for relaxation ('the Governor has returned fat as a seal,' George Myers reported irreverently to John Hardman after one such trip)[26] but chiefly to seek inspiration from the great Gothic architecture of northern Europe. Jane and Pugin honeymooned in England during their first summer together; the following year, Pugin went to the Continent by himself:

I cannot tell you how it grieves me to leave you. I wish you could always be with me & never away for a moment, but you know how it is necessary for me sometimes to get sketches or I should not be able to get on. … You are my only comfort & I think of you continually … Pray write me a few times every day. It is such a comfort to me. Be very careful and do not fatigue yourself – & let Mr. Powell sleep in the house.[27]

The next summer, in 1850, Pugin took Jane with him to France.

Despite his busyness and absences, Pugin's letters to Jane also reveal a close involvement with the daily functioning of The Grange. He is frequently involved in the hiring of servants and a letter written from Alton on 1st May 1850 typifies the tone and attention to detail in his letters as well as his personal piety:

As this is the month of May, I hope you will see proper devotions kept up. The tapers lit every evening in the hall before the image, lights & flowers before the image in the chapel [at The Grange] on benediction. The magnificat said or sung every evening in the little chapel with the prayer sub tuum praesidium & c. & ora pro nobis & at the end. The litany of the B[lessed] Virgin sung at Benediction on Thursday … Kisses for little Margaret, love to all. God bless you, my own. Flowers before image in hall.[28]

In the early pages of the journal, which are written a little stiffly, it is not easy to catch a sense of Jane's personality. The accounts are interesting as much for being the voice of a Victorian middle-class wife and mother. She is ever discreet, describing going into labour as feeling 'very ill' or 'rather ill'. When her servants let her down, running the household of eight children cannot have been easy. No doubt the young men employed to work on designs for stained glass windows in the Cartoon Room in the north courtyard at The Grange were also in and out of the house but Jane never complains. There were also times of worry and insecurity: her husband's gradually declining health, for example, or the anti-Catholic feeling that boiled over into disturbances in the town on 5th November 1850. Pugin himself was extremely concerned for the physical security at The Grange, barring all doors at 10.30 p.m. on the dot.

That Jane was physically very attractive is clear from her portrait and perhaps especially from surviving photographs. As a young woman, she smiles out enigmatically with an expression both warm and intelligent (Figs 2 & 11) and in old age, no less beautiful, she has the dignity of a matriarch (Fig. 13). Ralph Neville, a later apologist for the Victorian Age, describes her as 'a very pretty woman and [she] had something of the appearance of some mediaeval beauty transferred to modern times.'[29] With a poignant irony, as far as the journal is concerned, her personality emerges most clearly when she is writing of Pugin's last months, when she remains steadfastly resourceful and courageous through events that must have been almost unbearable for her.

Mrs. Pugin was enthusiastic in her love of ancient art, and appreciating her husband's genius entered into all his projects. When his health gave way, she watched over him with the most affectionate care. He often refers in his letters to the soothing manner in which she nursed him when he was suffering intense pain.[30]

Pugin had always had an inclination to drive himself too hard and had suffered his first nervous collapse in his twenties. As he grew older, he habitually took mercury, believed to be a remedy for inflamed eyes but, as we now know, also highly and cumulatively toxic. Today, mercury is notoriously known as an early remedy for syphilis and some

Fig. 10
Augustus Pugin on the Albert Memorial. George Gilbert Scott has modestly
relegated himself to the bas relief profile behind Pugin's shoulder.
(*Caroline Stanford*)

have mischievously imputed that this lay behind Pugin's doses.[31] In fact, mercury was prescribed for a number of other symptoms and illnesses in apparent ignorance of its potentially lethal accumulation in the body. The acute observer did perhaps make the connection between supposed remedy and further decline: in 1811, Dr Andrew Mathias, the Surgeon Extraordinary to the Queen, wrote that 'we do not find any author who uniformly imputes this change [i.e. an intensified decline during the treatment of VD] to one true specific disease from the effects of mercury only.'[32] He proceeds to list in his treatise the side effects of the condition he called mercurial disease, noting, 'Mercury appears to destroy the energy of the nervous system, producing weakness, tremors, palsies, fatuity, epilepsy and mania, the most dreadful of all its bad consequences; and indeed no part of the body is exempt from its deleterious effects.'[33]

Abraham Lincoln was prescribed mercury pills to counteract depression, but he took himself off the substance when he realised it made him liable to violent mood swings. Pugin seems never to have made this connection between his erratic health and the long-term effects of his supposed medicine and nor did his doctors or any of those around him. In September 1841, for example, Pugin's eyes were so inflamed that he wrote to his friend John Rouse Bloxam that 'the surgeons declared that in a few hours the sight of one if not both eyes would have been irrecoverably lost.'[34] On 29th September he wrote to Lord Shrewsbury:

I avail myself of the blessing of returning sight to write as soon as possible … My eyes are still weak and I am much reduced … I was obliged to take 3 grains of mercury every 4 hours for *some time* to drive out the inflammation & my teeth are quite Lossened [*sic*] and I have great pains in all my limbs. I am now taking medicine to remove the effect of the mercury. I have indeed suffered dreadfully.[35]

Cumulatively, doses of mercury at such levels would be sufficiently toxic to ensure severe poisoning. His ill health was not continuous but could be crippling; in 1846 he wrote to his friend Henry Drummond complaining of 'dreadful nervous fevers', his eyes so bad he could hardly write.[36] He was virtually confined to his house and saw nobody. At times like these he depended upon Hardman Powell and later Jane to act as his amanuensis for his many letters to suppliers and clients.

Pugin had frequent intimations of his own mortality and hated the thought of dying in debt. In his letters to his decorator Crace, for example, mention of bouts of ill health is typically accompanied either by payment or a request that Crace let him know what he owes:

> I am very anxious now to have the accounts for all things that we may yet spend. I am very unwell indeed & dread the idea of dying in debt. It disturbs me.[37]

On 10th November 1848, four months after his marriage to Jane and perhaps prompted by it, Pugin notes in his diary 'Insured my life for £2,000 in the Victoria.'

Pugin's letters provide perhaps the best record of his life, but when these dried up as he entered the final months of his illness, Jane's journal becomes a crucial source. Pugin records his own decline in a poignant series of letters written in January 1852 about his accounts to Minton, reproduced by both Ferrey and Trappes-Lomax. Jane and indeed Pugin's own friends were too discreet (and perhaps too loyal) to go into such details about the symptoms he suffered and the medical records after his committal to

Bedlam are terse.[38] Pugin, however, writes in his own extremity:

> Pray, my dear Minton, don't agitate me, the doctors say I am not to be agitated. If you saw your poor friend so reduced as I am – thin, trembling, hollow-eyed, changed and yet working tremendously at times – you would be careful not to distress me.[39] ... you have no conception of the dreadful agony which I still suffer, the least thing agitates me; I feel trembling and my eyesight is dimmed. I am obliged to bathe my eyes with sea water, and to drink the coldest water to bring my sight again.[40]

And finally on 16th February 1852, again to Minton:

> After I wrote to you I was taken with a terrible relapse and a *stagnation of the blood*. I soon became cold in all the vital parts, and I felt that without instant relief I must die. I ordered three strong glasses of brandy: - my doctor came in: - and by the mercy of God, and by about half a pint of sal volatile which I drank off, and by my dear wife putting hot flannels all over me, with rubbing, in which others assisted, at last the circulation returned. My medical man said this could not go on any longer, and he had a consultation of all the first medical men, who declared that I could not live a week if I did not give up my profession. There was no hesitation on my part: I immediately relinquished all my buildings except Lord Shrewsbury's and Sir C. Barry's, and of course yours, which will not kill me; but I am a private gentleman, a grand fellow. The relief of mind, as the doctors predicted, was instantaneous and succeeded perfectly, and I am, thank God out of danger ... My mind has been deranged through over exertion. The medical men said I had worked one hundred years in forty. I have not time to say more: I am ordered to Italy as soon as possible.[41]

Sadly, there were to be no more excursions to the Continent for Pugin. On 25th February he went to London on business with Edward. His condition worsened and two days later he was taken to Kensington House, a private mental asylum. When his condition failed to improve, he was moved on 21st June to Bedlam, a public asylum chiefly for paupers although also offering excellent medical care. Through these events, the menfolk of Pugin's circle – John Hardman, George Myers, John Herbert, John Knill and Edward Pugin – kept Jane very much at arm's length. She seems not to have been allowed to visit her husband from February until June. The story unfolds in Jane's journal, but it is an interesting illustration of a patriarchal society 'protecting' an intelligent and resourceful young woman from a situation she subsequently proved herself capable of managing with dignity and courage. Her insistence that her husband be moved first from Bedlam to a private house and eventually back to his own home in Ramsgate for his final few days and her nursing of him reveal deep compassion and love.

There was also a sense in which the nation was watching Pugin's final demise. The triumphs of Pugin's work on the Mediaeval Court at the Great Exhibition and at the House of Lords meant that he was well-known and regarded regardless of the religious controversy he undoubtedly courted. On 2nd September 1852, less than two weeks before his death, Jane was granted a Civil List pension of £100 per annum, 'In consideration of her husband's eminence as an Architect, and the distressed situation in which his family are placed, from his inability, in consequence of illness, to pursue his profession. In trust to John Hardman, Esq., and John Knill, Esq.'[42] According to Ferrey, the pension was 'communicated to Mrs. Pugin, in the most complimentary manner by the Earl of Derby',[43]

Fig. 11

A family group, possibly a photomontage, *c.*1851. Jane is seated at the front with (left to right) 17-year-old Edward, Anne (in a bonnet as perhaps befitted her newly married status) and 15-year-old Agnes. The group may have been taken to mark the Great Exhibition in 1851, as Jane appears to be wearing the parure given to Pugin at their marriage and displayed in the Mediaeval Court at the Crystal Palace.

(*Private collection*)

Fig. 12
Sketch of young woman nursing a child with young boy,
by A. W. Pugin *c*.1849. The enigmatic smile of the young
woman in this intimate sketch makes her recognisably
Jane, probably nursing Margaret.
(*Victoria & Albert Museum Drawings Collection*)

Fig. 13
Family group, *c.*1900. A serene matriarch, Jane is seated second from the left, next to her son Peter Paul Pugin (the other sitters have yet to be identified). Jane was to die at the age of 84 in 1909, a widow for more than fifty years.
(*Purcell Collection, RIBA*)

but it is perhaps a further example of the male hegemony in Victorian society that the pension was to be held in trust by her uncle and Hardman despite her years.

On 14th September 1852, Pugin died and Jane was left a widow of 27 with eight dependent children. His wish was that everything be left to Jane, including the responsibility of what should be given to each child. Pugin had left as his will a scrap of paper sealed in an envelope, dated 11th May 1850. There is nothing in his diary to suggest what may have prompted Pugin to draw up his will, although he did depart for a tour of northern France and Germany on 14th May 1850:

> +Ramsgate May 11th 1850
> 'I hereby bequeath to my dear wife Jane Pugin the whole of my property of whatsoever description I am possessed of to dispose of as she thinks meet [?] for the benefit of herself and my children – and in this disposition it is my express wish and desire that she should consult it [sic] John Hardman of Birmingham and act with his concurrence.
> & I hereby appoint the aforesaid Jane Pugin and John Hardman goldsmith of Birmingham to be the executors to this my last will and testament. Witness my hand & seal
> +Augustus Northmore Welby Pugin
> Witness +John Hardman Powell'[44]

However, as the will was witnessed by a single witness only, Pugin had effectively died intestate. Under the law of gavelkind that then applied, Jane, who was given administration of the estate, was left with no alternative but to liquidate her husband's collection of books, paintings and *objets d'art* to meet her obligations. The sales took place the following spring, yielding disappointing totals and, while an auction sets its own values, Jane's sense of outrage at the bargains picked up by Pugin's friends and relations is clear.

Next came the problem of where the family should live. The journal reveals an apparent and rather unseemly wish on the part of both John Knill and John Hardman to avoid responsibility for the family, each urging Jane instead to live close to the other. In the event, she decided to follow Edward to Birmingham in order to keep the family together and it is at the point of this decision that the journal ends. The move had a logic to it beyond Jane's financial links with Hardman through her State pension, since it enabled Edward, now acquiring status as an architect in his own right, to work closely with Hardman & Co. The Grange was rented out to Pugin's good friend, Alfred Luck, but the complex of house, church and monastery that constitute St Augustine's, begun by Pugin, exerted a strong pull on the family. In 1858, Edward returned to Ramsgate to continue work on the church and local commissions soon followed. After a brief period in Gordon Square, Bloomsbury, Edward, Jane and the other unmarried children returned to The Grange in 1861.

It became once more a family home, although of a slightly different character from its inception under Augustus. This was now a family of adults, not children, and a family more comfortable with its role in local society. The simple, rather austere life lived there by Pugin, with his books and library and Christian architecture by the sea, gave way to the needs of a household adapting to the comforts of the Victorian bourgeoisie. Edward no longer worked in the library off his own drawing room as his father had done, but, rather, established a studio in St Edward's Presbytery, adjacent on the site. He had a close relationship with Jane, who he described as 'one of the best mothers any man could be blessed with.'[45] The family became more confident about taking its place in the town than in Augustus's day in a manner that seems a far cry from Jane's alarm at the anti-

Catholic disturbances in November 1850. The family remained devoutly Catholic but society was changing and becoming more genuinely tolerant of religious differences. In 1862, the *Thanet Advertiser* reported in glowing terms on a dinner at The Grange at which Cardinal Wiseman was entertained, commenting especially on 'the rare tact and charming manners of the hostess.'[46] Edward soon established himself as something of a local figure, particularly in the local militia and Jane too became a well-liked and respected figure in the town. At the ball held to celebrate the wedding of her stepdaughter Mary Pugin in 1867, Jane again got a special mention in the press:

> We cannot help noticing the appearance of Mrs Welby Pugin: she was attired in a dress of white satin embroidered with Gothic ornamentation in gold, fastened with studs of gold, richly jewelled and confined at the waist with a girdle splendidly enamelled with the devices of the Knill family. Over this she wore a mantle of blue velvet lined with white silk, and clasped at the shoulder with a Gothic brooch set with jewels.[47]

Jane never married again, and lived until 1909. The intervening years brought their toll: Edward filed for bankruptcy in 1872 and died aged only forty-one three years later after a life hardly longer than his father's. Jane outlived both her own children (Margaret died in her thirties in 1884 and Peter Paul in 1904) and all her stepchildren save Cuthbert, Mary and Catherine. Cuthbert never married and remained at The Grange with his stepmother, although by the end of the century the house was largely let out to summer visitors for extra income, Jane and Cuthbert living instead in the adjacent St Edward's Presbytery. In 1904, Jane witnessed a near disastrous fire at

The Grange. Yet the voice that speaks through the journal suggests that Jane had the strength and resilience to weather such storms. Of the two verses she inscribed at the very end of her journal, in a later version of her hand, the first expresses the loyalty she kept throughout her life to the husband she adored. The second, dated 'Ramsgate 1876', perhaps sums up her approach to life and strength in her own femininity and also has a sense of resilience and perhaps even exhilaration from, by then, a 50-year-old woman: 'Give me but my Freedom & my Health/The Sum of my Desire!' It is the cry of woman who revels in her own independence and Jane was lucky enough to enjoy both health and freedom for most of her long life. Her husband may have measured her by the standards of earlier ages and valued Jane as 'a first-rate Gothic woman' but she also had many qualities that, from our later age, we may appraise as thoroughly modern. It is this sense of empathy that makes Jane's journal such compelling reading.

Notes

1 W. A. Wickham, article in *Transactions of the Historical Society of Lancashire and Cheshire,* new series, vol. 23, cited in M. Trappes-Lomax, *Pugin: A Medieval Victorian* (1932), p. 280, n. 2.

2 Letter to John Rouse Bloxam, 13th September 1840 (Magdalen College, Oxford, MS 528/8, reproduced in Margaret Belcher, *The Collected Letters of A. W. N. Pugin*, vol. 1 (2001), p. 144. Thanks to Timothy Brittain-Catlin for retrieving the source of this famous passage.

3 There seems nevertheless to have been some affection between them; Trappes-Lomax relates that she later married a rich man and left money to Pugin's children from his first two marriages (p. 280).

4 Alexandra Wedgwood, 'Pugin in his Home: A Memoir by J. H. Powell', *Architectural History,* 31 (1988), p. 174 and n. 7.

5 HLRO, Hist. Coll. 339/130 (n.d.).

6 HLRO, Hist. Coll. 339/125 (n.d.).

7 HRLO, Hist. Coll. 339/133 (n.d.).

8 Benjamin Ferrey, *Recollections of A. W. N. Pugin and his Father Augustus Pugin* (1861), p. 213.

9 Michael Egan, 'Mrs Jane Pugin and some London Relations', *True*

Principles, 2 no. 4 (Summer 2002), p. 22.

10 See Paul Atterbury and Clive Wainwright (editors), *Pugin: A Gothic Passion* (1994), p. 173.

11 Alexandra Wedgwood, *A. W. N. Pugin and the Pugin Family: Catalogues of Architectural Drawings in the Victoria and Albert Museum* (1985), p. 64.

12 Ibid., **73**, p. 115.

13 Bernard Bogan, *The Great Link: A History of St. George's Southwark* (1948), p. 146.

14 Ferrey, p. 231.

15 HLRO, Hist. Coll. 339/125 (n.d.).

16 Ferrey, p. 221.

17 See Atterbury and Wainwright, p. 169. The jewellery is now at the Victoria and Albert Museum.

18 Wedgwood (1988), p. 175. This account by John Hardman Powell gives a vivid picture of Pugin and of daily life at The Grange.

19 Ibid., p. 190.

20 HLRO, Hist. Coll. 339/132 (n.d.). In the same letter Pugin writes that all his children had measles. It must have been chaos.

21 Wedgwood (1988), p. 193.

22 For example: 'During this, his second visit to the Manor, he begged us to pay him one at the new house he had just finished at Ramsgate, now called The Grange, it would give us new ideas in furniture and other details. Consequently, my Uncle, Mother and myself went there for two days at the end of summer. The Church was not yet begun but the house was simply perfect. A statue of the Blessed Virgin and Divine Infant was the first object seen on entering the hall, the oaken staircase was painted with inscriptions of welcome; even the silver candlesticks, the teapots and every article of plate had their inscriptions, giving life and soul to the whole building and true to the conception of a Christian architect he received us in his robe of office, a kind of cassock copied from old pictures which he always wore within his own precincts. Two delighted days we spent there despite bad weather, studying his large collection of beautiful sketches, whilst each morning he worked at designs that were urgent and for which he laughingly told us would bring £100 [*sic?*: this figure is not very clearly written]. But one most unexpected feature in the dwelling were luxurious and easy chairs of the most modern upholstery besides, while the mullioned windows showed plate glass beneath, the upper windows were of coloured designs. This was apparently in direct contradiction for diamond panes and high backed chairs of Elizabethan pattern, but in reality it only showed the combination of practical good sense and high ideas which differentiated him from common men.' Quoted from Winifrede M. Wyse, Reminiscences of Augustus Welby Pugin (HLRO, PUG 3/13/348 (n.d.). It seems likely that Winifrede's uncle was the Mr

Wyse whose house Pugin includes in a list of his work in Ireland – see Wedgwood (1985), **96**, p. 121.

23 HLRO, PUG 3/7/294 (n.d.). Margaret Belcher's third volume of *The Collected Letters of A. W. N. Pugin* will cover the years of his marriage to Jane.

24 Wedgwood (1985), **75**, p.116.

25 Ibid., **79**, p. 117.

26 Patricia Spencer-Silver, *Pugin's Builder: The Life and Works of George Myers* (1993), p. 74.

27 Wedgwood (1985), **80**, p. 117. Written from Boulogne on 24th August 1849 when Jane was pregnant with Margaret.

28 Ibid., **83**, p. 117. Margaret was seven months old.

29 Ralph Neville, *The Gay Victorians* (1930), p. 117.

30 Ferrey, p. 230.

31 See, for example, Guy R. Williams, *Augustus Pugin versus Decimus Burton: An Architectural Duel* (1990).

32 Andrew Mathias, *The Mercurial Disease* (1811), p.17.

33 Ibid., p. 19.

34 Belcher, vol. 1, p. 272.

35 Ibid., p. 275.

36 Drummond Papers (Alnwick Castle), C/17/42, cited by Spencer-Silver, p. 74.

37 RIBA, PUG/CRACE 1/33, 1844.

38 See Margaret Belcher, *Pugin: An Annotated Critical Bibliography* (1987), pp. 317-19.

39 Ferrey, p. 253.

40 Ibid., p. 265.

41 Ibid., pp. 265-6.

42 Parliamentary Papers: HC 1852-3 (682), LVII, p. 353.

43 Ferrey, p. 274.

44 HLRO, PUG 3/9/11/322 (n.d.).

45 *Kent Coast Times*, 18th August 1870, cited by Catriona Blaker in *Edward Pugin and Kent* (2003), p. 4.

46 Blaker, p. 16.

47 *Thanet Advertiser*, 30th November 1867, cited in ibid., p. 17.

My Journal from the year
I was Married.

Aug.t 18th I was married at
St George's Church by Dr Doyle
the head chaplain there were present my Husband, Uncle, Haile
& Aunt. Annie Edward & Cyril
Anjim. Mr Herbert R.A. Rev. &c.
J. Telford (to whom I made my general confession) Tabot. Cotter
after Mass at which we receive
the most Holy Communion we
returned to Welworth House
at ½ past 9 and breakfasted
we left there for the railway
at ½ past 11 and arrived
at Ramsgate at ½ past 3 o'clk
the flag was hoisted for the first
time. Cuthbert. Catherine and
Mary, with Sarah & Mary the
servants were ready to receive

JANE PUGIN'S JOURNAL

♦ ♦ ♦

[Jane Pugin writes with very little punctuation, which has been inserted in transcription where this facilitates comprehension.]

My journal from the year I was married [1848]

August 10th. I was married at St George's Church[1] by Dr Doyle[2] the head Chaplain. There were present my

---

[1] St George's, Southwark, was designed by Pugin after a limited competition, an important and prominent commission. At first the authorities had been reluctant to sell any land for such a purpose but they eventually agreed to sell the plot on St George's Road for £3,200. Their conditions were that the church should be built to Pugin's design and could have 'no ecclesiastical ornament on the outside.' The first stone was laid in 1840 and John Knill and his son Stuart were key benefactors in the building's construction. The church opened on 4th July 1848 in the presence of thirteen bishops and 250 clergy – the largest number of Catholic priests to have assembled in one place in England since the Reformation (Alexandra Wedgwood, *A. W. N. Pugin and the Pugin Family, Catalogues of Architectural Drawings in the Victoria and Albert Museum* (1985), **18** p. 96, and see Patricia Spencer-Silver, *Pugin's Builder: The Life and Work of George Myers* (1993), pp. 53-7 for a detailed account of the construction of St George's). In 1850, when Pope Pius IX restored the English Catholic Hierarchy, St George's was chosen as the Cathedral Church of the Diocese of Southwark, covering the whole of southern England. Until Westminster Cathedral opened

husband, Uncle Knill & Aunt, Annie, Edward & Agnes Pugin, Mr. Herbert R.A.,[3] Revd. J. Telford (to whom I made my general Confession),[4] Talbot,[5] Cotter[?]. After Mass at which we received the most Holy Communion, we returned to Walworth House at 1/2 past 9 and breakfasted. We left there for the railway at 1/2 past 11 and arrived at Ramsgate at 1/2 past 3 o'clock. The flag was hoisted for the first time. Cuthbert, Catherine and Mary, with Sarah & Mary the servants, were ready to receive us at the front door. Had dinner, roast fowls and cherry & currant tarts. The 3 oldest returned from my Aunt's on the Saturday (as I was married on the Thursday). We remained at home a fortnight. We then travelled for 5 weeks up the East Coast

---

some fifty years later, St George's was the centre of Catholic life in England. It was bombed during the Second World War and, though rebuilt, very little remains of the original as designed by Pugin. Pugin's own diary records for this day 'United to my dearest Jane at St George's and on to Ramsgate.'

[2] Dr Thomas Doyle (1793-1879) was a charismatic priest who came to the earlier church of St George's in 1820 when it had a congregation of 7,000. By the time the Catholic Emancipation Act was passed in 1829, the congregation had swelled to 15,000 and the idea grew in Dr Doyle's mind of a great church, large enough to be a cathedral. Dr Doyle was considered particularly bold in his promotion of the open veneration of the Virgin Mary (Spencer-Silver, p. 54).

[3] John Rogers Herbert R.A., had converted to Catholicism around 1840 and became a close friend of Pugin's. He was a frequent visitor to The Grange and painted Pugin in 1845. He is also thought to have painted Jane, although her portrait has since disappeared. His well-known portrait of Pugin now hangs in the Pugin Room at the House of Commons, together with a portrait of Jane painted by G. A. Freezor in 1859.

[4] The Rev. John Telford (1814-65) served as priest in St George's in the 1840s (Michael Egan, 'Mrs Jane Pugin and some London Relations', *True Principles*, 2 no. 4 (Summer 2002), p. 24).

[5] Perhaps Thomas Talbot Bury (1811-77), an architect who had been a pupil of Pugin's father, A.C. Pugin and therefore knew Augustus well. According to Hardman Powell, 'There were days of laughter when he came' and he would tease Pugin about having slept in the boxes in the auditorium at Covent Garden during his brief career as a scene painter in his youth (A. Wedgwood, 'Pugin in his Home: A Memoir by J. H. Powell', *Architectural History*, 31 (1988), p. 191).

of England & so to Scotland up as far as Stirling. We then returned by the Lakes, down the West coast just through the North of Wales, then to Birmingham, Salisbury, to Winchester & then home where we found Dr. Walsh[6] & Dr. Moore[7] staying.[8] Agnes went to school at Caverswall Castle about the middle of October.

---

[6] Dr Thomas Walsh (1779-1849) was one of Pugin's most loyal supporters. He was President of St. Mary's College, Oscott near Birmingham from 1818 to 1826, after which he was appointed Bishop of the Midland District.

[7] Dr John Moore (1807-56) was appointed President of Oscott in 1848, a post he held until 1853, and was a good friend of John Hardman. Pugin carried out alterations to and the furnishing of the chapel at St Mary's College from 1837. The commissions at Oscott were crucial both in introducing Pugin to future patrons and in establishing his reputation within the Catholic Church in England.

[8] Pugin's own diary – rarely more than a terse record of where he had spent a particular day – gives a better idea of the punishing itinerary the newly-weds shared. Pugin was taking Jane to many of his favourite places and buildings; the names of several of the cathedrals they must have visited feature on the cornice frieze in the library at The Grange, the family home Pugin had built to live in with his second wife, Louisa Burton. Pugin liked to draw inspiration from the names of his favourite places and people as he worked. Unlike Jane's account, which is clearly retrospective in this section, Pugin probably made his diary entries on the same day. Various drawings and watercolours survive from this trip (see Wedgwood (1985), **21** p. 96). Their five-week wedding tour was as follows:

'August 11-14	Ramsgate,
	London to Cambridge, Ely, Wilburton
	Ely, Peterborough, Stamford
	Stamford, Melton, Grantham, Lincoln
	Lincoln
	Lincoln to Nottingham and back
	Lincoln, Boston, Wainflete, Skegness
	Skegness, Louth, Hull
	Hull, Beverley, Filey
September	Filey, Scarborough, Whitby
	Whitby
	Whitby to York
	York, Ripon, Durham
	Durham, Ushaw, Alnwick
	Alnwick, Warkworth, Belford
	Belford, Edinburgh, Roslin
	Edinburgh, Dundee, Perth, Sterling [sic]

Christmas day we had a large party. Thorntons,[9] Herberts, Lady Mostyn[10] & family, [-?-] [-?-] Peter & his wife, Mr. & Mrs. Tom Walmsley[11] & Mr & Mrs Richard Walsh, Mr & Mrs Michael Walmsley & their niece, Miss [-?-] & Bob[?] Walmsley. We enjoyed ourselves very much. On Twelfth Day still more fun – the same party with Mr Barry,[12] Mr Hardman[13] [-?-] [-?-] Daniels.[14] We drew characters. I was the Queen, Daniel was King, we passed a very pleasant evening [indecipherable phrase].[15]

Edinburgh to Carlisle and Kendal
Kendal, Windermere and back
Kendal to Liverpool
Liverpool to Chester, Holywell, Bangor, Caernarvon
Bangor to Lanwyst [sic], Chester
Chester to Lichfield and Birmingham
Bilton, Warwick, Kenilworth. Paid Myers
    the £50 he lent me on the 29th July
    [Pugin hated to have debts outstanding]
Birmingham
Birmingham
Birmingham to Wells, Gloucester
At Wells and Glastonbury
Wells to Dorchester
Dorchester to Salisbury
Salisbury to Winchester & London
London to Ramsgate'
(Wedgwood (1985), p. 64).

[9] The Thornton family were mill owners and lived at Sturry, a few miles from Ramsgate. They were among Pugin's closest friends and the children of both families played together. Ferrey gives Pugin's merry invitation to the Thorntons: 'The humble petition of the inhabitants and sojourners of St Augustine's, Ramsgate. Whereas on the Feast of the Epiphany forthcoming, commonly called Twelfth Day, divers revels are to be held at St. Augustine's; and whereas much of contentment and joy of the said revels would be lost if Mr. J. Thornton of Sturry be not present to assist thereat; the petitioners therefore most humbly pray that he will not fail to come, together with all belonging to him. God Save the Queen!
Signed, A. WELBY PUGIN, JANE PUGIN, E. B. DANIEL, KEZIA HER-BERT, ANNE PUGIN, J. R. HERBERT, J. H. POWELL, A. HERBERT, CUTHBERT W. PUGIN, CATHARINE PUGIN, MARY PUGIN,

EDWARD W. PUGIN, A. HERBERT.' (Ferrey, p. 181).

[10] Lady Mostyn, the Hon. Frances Georgina, wife of Sir Pyers Mostyn. The Mostyns were a local Catholic family. In 1864, Major Henry Mostyn, presumably a relation, was to endow a new Catholic church, St Henry and St Elizabeth in Sheerness to a design commissioned from Pugin's son Edward. Such examples of interconnection between Catholic families are not unusual (Catriona Blaker, *Edward Pugin and Kent* (2003), p. 30).

[11] Perhaps part of the same family as the Walmsleys of Wigan, to whom Pugin supplied a cross in 1850 (Wedgwood (1985), Diaries, 1850, *bep* [f].)

[12] Charles Barry (1795-1860), the architect of the Palace of Westminster with whom Pugin designed the interiors and fittings.

[13] John Hardman jnr (1812-67) was the son of John Hardman (d. 1844) who had had a successful business manufacturing metal buttons in Birmingham. In 1838, Pugin persuaded Hardman jnr to make his ecclesiastical metalwork and the business grew rapidly. From 1845 Hardman also produced stained glass to Pugin's designs. Hardman was one of a small band of colleagues who supplied the bedrock of Pugin's genius by executing the drawings that flowed from his pen. J. G. Crace, his decorator, and George Myers, his builder, completed this triumvirate.

[14] James Daniel was a good friend of Pugins and the family doctor, practising from the High Street in Ramsgate. Says Hardman Powell' '[Daniel] came frequently and Pugin and he had merry talks about all that was going on in the world.' (Wedgwood (1988), p. 190).

[15] Christmas 1848 must have been one of the happiest at The Grange. There are two other accounts of it. On 26th December, Pugin wrote to his patron, Lord Shrewsbury: 'we have Lady Mostyn here and [the] Honble Mr Petre & several Catholics who come to reside for the winter & are delighted with the functions at the Church. We had a magnificent service for midnight mass, the whole church draped with holly & brilliant with tapers. We had a feast afterwards & solemn vespers in the house on Xmas Day, a Catholic party, with a good Xmas tree & everybody was delighted. We have really now a very edifying congregation. My wife manages everything most admirably & is a great comfort and assistance to me.' (Wedgwood, (1985), **63**, L.525 – 1965, p. 113). And John Hardman Powell wrote: 'Every year he [Pugin] had a Xmass tree and on one Twelfth day, in honour of his marriage a huge Cake with St. George and dragon modelled especially, and many of his guests took characters, wearing badges drawn by himself; he kept all alive by his wit and evident enjoyment, but at ten-thirty "douse the glims and clear decks", and not a remnant of festivity was left for morning.' (Wedgwood (1988), p. 178).

[1849]

May, we went up to London to my Aunt at Walworth House, bought baby linen.[16] I saw Mrs Thomas but she was engaged. Went about every night to the Opera with which I was much pleased, as I had never been allowed to go before I was married.

June Mrs Powell came down on a visit to her son [John Hardman Powell]. Mr Cormick[?] from [-?-] came down on a visit. Agnes came home from school for the holidays.

21st of June. My birthday. We went to Richborough Castle near Sandwich for a Pick Nick. Dearest Augustus was out sketching, just as we were going to dine he came quite unexpectedly which made us spend a very happy day.[17] Augustus went out sketching the Kentish Churches almost all this summer, many days walking 18 or 20 miles besides taking 5 or 6 coloured sketches. He was never idle, he never wasted a moment. On the 10th of August my wedding day the Feast of St. Lawrence we had another Pick Nick which we enjoyed much.[18] Part of us went on Donkeys and part in Donkey carriages. Cuthbert and Catherine[19] were in a little carriage by themselves. The reins of the donkey broke, they were very nearly going down a dyke but Cuthbert jumped out behind first, followed by Kathy. It was rather an amusing sight. Still I was much frightened for fear they might be hurt. Edward, Mr. Powell & Cuthbert had to run home on account of it being the evening for Benediction.

---

[16] Pugin recorded 'May 21 – Ramsgate to London with dearest Jane.' They returned to Ramsgate on 26th May (Wedgwood (1985), p. 66).

[17] Pugin noted 'June 21 – Ash, Sandwich and Rack[?] Richborough. Dearest Jane's birthday.' (Ibid.).

[18] This entry implies that Pugin was with Jane on their first wedding anniversary. In fact, according to his own diary, he was in Edinburgh on 10th August. His work always came first.

[19] Cuthbert and Catherine were Pugin's fourth and fifth children respectively, their mother being Louisa Burton.

About the 14th of October dearest Augustus had to leave home on business.[20] Mr. Powell then came to remain with me and on the 17th October at 1/2 past 7pm I was taken very ill. Mr. Daniel sent for. At 10 minutes past 12 at night dear little Margaret was born.[21] My dear husband came home the next day.

On the Sunday following, she was Baptized, my Aunt Mrs. Knill standing Godmother and Stuart Knill my cousin stood proxy Godfather for my Uncle Mr. John Knill.[22] Revd. Thomas Costogan[23] baptized her in the little chapel in the house as she was very delicate. Mrs. Handford was the monthly nurse. During the month dear little Margaret had a swelling on her left breast, it was lanced and afterwards it got quite well. I had a nurse in the house, an Irish girl of the

---

[20] Despite the fact that Jane was pregnant, Pugin kept up his usual heavy work schedule: his diary reveals him to have been in Scotland, Ireland and France through the summer. This particular trip on 14th was no doubt noted by Jane because she was so near term, and similarly the fact that John Powell, a young bachelor of 22, was left to keep an eye on her as Pugin's assistant.

[21] Pugin recorded 'October 17 – Burlington to Cambridge. Dear little Margaret born at ? past 12am.' However, according to his diary, he did not return to Ramsgate until 20th October. (Wedgwood, 1985, p. 67). Margaret (1849-84) was Pugin's seventh child. She married first Henry Francis Purcell (d. 1877) and their son Charles Henry Cuthbert Purcell (1874-1958) was the last member of the architectural firm of Pugin & Pugin, founded by Augustus's sons Edward, Cuthbert and Peter Paul.

[22] John Knill was Jane's adoptive father as well as her uncle, and Stuart was his son. The Knills hailed from Herefordshire and converted to the Catholic faith in 1842. Both John and Stuart were active in the City of London and Stuart was to become Lord Mayor of London in 1892 – an illustration of greater religious tolerance as the century drew to a close. Both were also active members of St George's, Southwark and contributed towards the new church built by Pugin. When John died in 1854, Stuart commissioned Edward Pugin to design the Knill chantry chapel there.

[23] Jane consistently misspells this name, which should be Father Costigan. Costigan was priest at Margate, the nearest Catholic church to The Grange until St Augustine's opened in 1850. According to Hardman Powell, 'He had a large kindly nature in a large frame, and 75 miles of coast to walk to find his flock' (Wedgwood (1988), p. 191).

name of Maria. She was my Aunt's maid before I was married. She wished much to come to me so I engaged her the very day Mrs. Handford left. This Maria soon gave me notice to leave. I was much annoyed with her so I gave her a month's wages and told her she was to leave the next day but one.[24] I was then left without a nurse so I took a young girl of 15 to take charge of baby.[25] I had therefore to attend entirely to her myself which certainly made me very ill. I continued in this way for five months. Augustus then engaged a nurse who had lived at the Ryders' then Philippe's cousins. Her name was Ann Slater.[26] We called her Lucy, she came in May 1850. She was good-looking but too forward. She used to give Margaret sugar at night which made her teeth black. This I did not find out til after she left.[27] Sarah the cook who had lived in the family for 9 years left and went to live with Mr. Hardman in Handsworth, Birmingham.[28]

[1850]

I weaned Margaret about this time after nursing her for 6 months. She was indeed a dear, pretty little thing. Annie[29]

[24] Pugin noted at Ramsgate 'November 23 – Maria left. Heavy gale ship on the sand.' (Wedgwood (1985), p. 67).

[25] Pugin noted 'November 24 – Girl from Mrs. Wal…[?] came.' (Ibid.).

[26] Pugin is the one who engaged Lucy – he writes to his wife 'she is very good looking which I know is a point with you. I mean good holy looking. I deem[?] she is a very holy person.' (HLRO, PUG 3/6/195). He records her eventual arrival on April 18th 1850 (Wedgwood (1985), p. 68).

[27] Lucy seems to have left in disgrace. Pugin wrote to Jane from Belgium on 29th July, 1851: 'I have just arrived at Antwerp and got all your letters. I am greatly astonished about that appreciation from Lucy. What can it mean? I thought the man had run away from his wife & was going to take care of her. The whole thing seems mysterious - & I think you must not take notice of it but merely write what she was in your service.' (Ibid., **91**, p. 120).

[28] Pugin notes Sarah's departure on 21st March 1850 (ibid., p. 68).

[29] Presumably Pugin's eldest child, Anne (1832–97). Kathy (or Cathy) was his fifth child by Louisa Burton. She lived from 1841 until 1907.

taught Kathy and Polly: they were very good children and Father Costogan taught Edward and Cuthy. My dear Husband went abroad this year through the North of Germany. He was not well on his return, he had overworked himself during his journey. He brought home a quantity of most valuable sketches.[30]

After being abroad about a month, this was about July 1850, in August 1850 we had service in the Church for the first time on the Feast of the Assumption 15th August.[31] Every thing was done very quietly as my husband disliked any show or parade about such things. Anne Pugin my Husband's eldest daughter was married to Mr John Hardman Powell (nephew of Mr. John Hardman of Birmingham) October 1850.[32] This was the first marriage celebrated in the Church. Mrs. Powell Mr. Powell's Mother was the only one of his family present at the wedding. After breakfast they left by railroad for Maidstone. They only remained 3 days as the weather was so dreadfully wet. On

[30] According to his own diary, Pugin travelled from Ramsgate to Paris on 14th May, then over the next three weeks visited Chartres, Amiens, Brussels, Ghent, Tournai, Liège, Cologne, Minden, Hanover, Bremen, Hildesheim, Brunswick, Hamburg, Lübeck, Münster, Antwerp and Bruges before returning to Ramsgate on 4th June. He makes no mention of illness but on such a gruelling itinerary, it is not surprising that he returned exhausted. These trips abroad were not holidays for Pugin but would be dedicated to drawing and sketching the churches and cathedrals that he saw, to fuel his imagination when he returned home.

[31] Pugin's diary records this as taking place on 14th August ('St. Augustine's blessed and mass sung' – Wedgwood (1985), p. 69). He continues to record work to St Augustine's until February 1852. His son Edward was to continue the work.

[32] Anne (1832-97) was Pugin's eldest daughter by his first wife, Anne Garnet (?1811-32). John Hardman Powell (1827-95) was John Hardman's nephew and had lived at The Grange since 1844 as Pugin's assistant. He left lively accounts of his memories of life at The Grange in the 1840s (see Wedgwood (1988), pp. 171-201). Anne and John's marriage took place on 21st October 1850 according to Pugin's diary. The couple eventually settled in Birmingham where Powell became chief stained glass designer at Hardman's factory.

their return they went to their house which was ready for them at No. 3 Southwood Terrace, St. Lawrence.[33]

At Christmas we had our usual festivities but there were not so many invited consequently not so merry.[34] In this year Hierarchy was established which caused the awful No Popery row. I also forgot to say that on the 5th of Nov. 1850 the No Popery row in Ramsgate was fearful in the evening. The mob were coming to our house with the effigy of the Pope but they were turned back by the police. I was much frightened being not well at the time. My Husband was away.[35] Mr. & Mrs. Lewis were here that evening. Fortunately everything passed off very quietly.

1851

During the session Parlament [sic] taken up discussing the Ecclesiastical Titles Bill. Parlament was prorogued in Feby it was the[n] that my beloved Husband wrote that celebrated Pamphlet on the Hierarchy that made such a fearful noise in the world, it was most splendidly written but his views were not thoroughly understood: it was this which caused the row.[36] I forgot to say that in 1850 about the month of June dearest Augustus and I went to Paris for a few days.[37] I paid a visit to the nuns at the Convent of Sacre Coeur. I saw Madame d'Avena[?] and Madame Davidoff, after remaining 2 or 3 days in Paris we went to Bourges. We remained there 3 days, I was never in such a dirty place in

[33] Pugin seems to have helped furnish their new house, according to a sheet among his letters to his decorator, J. G. Crace (RIBA, PUG/CRACE 7/54), which is annotated on the reverse '1850 - plan of rooms at Ramsgate' and carries notes on wallpaper designs, colours and curtain fabrics. The measured room plans it shows do not correlate with those at The Grange and it seems likely that it relates instead to Southwood Terrace. (I am grateful to Paul Drury for this suggested attribution).

[34] Pugin's diary has no entry for Christmas 1850.

[35] Pugin was in Birmingham and makes no mention of this event.

my life. I believe we were in the Hotel de France, a most filthy place, the food was disgusting, this was considered the best hotel in the place. The Cathedral and the house which belonged to Jacques Coeur were beautiful besides many other things, this is why dearest Augustus remained there. From Bourges we went to Amiens for the Sunday, the service at the Cathedral was very fine. After Mass we saw the Vicar General, he was very kind. The next day we went all over the Cathedral with the [-?-] who knew my husband very well. He was consequently delighted to see us. We put up in the Hotel des Postes, a very nice clean house, in fact the nicest Hotel that we had been in since we left England.

---

[36] In 1850 Pope Pius IX re-established the Roman Catholic Hierarchy in England by subdividing the country into papal dioceses. Pugin was overjoyed and published a pamphlet entitled *An Earnest Address on the Establishment of the Catholic Hierarchy* urging his co-religionists to give the new episcopacy the spiritual and temporal support they required and, specifically, 5% of their income. Not surprisingly perhaps, this was not a popular suggestion. Pugin's diary for February 1851 notes : '16th Sent MSS to Dolman £20; 21st Sent part of MSS corrected; 26th ... Pamphlets published.' (Wedgwood (1985), p. 71). Pugin was presumably financing the publication himself but it had little effect. See Benjamin Ferrey, *Recollections of A. W. N. Pugin and his Father Augustus Pugin* (1861), pp. 295-303 for the full text of the pamphlet and a discussion of its impact, also David Meara's essay, 'The Catholic Context' in Atterbury (1995), p. 59. The general public regarded such initiatives from Rome with deep suspicion, interpreting them as potentially striking at the heart of the Anglican Church. Such fears among the general populace lay behind the periodic unrest on 5th November, the traditional celebration of Parliament's escape from so-called wicked Papists.

[37] Pugin gives their itinerary as 8th July Ramsgate to Boulogne; 9th Boulogne to Paris; 10th Paris; 11th Paris to Bourges; 12th Bourges; 13th Bourges to Paris & Amiens; 14th Amiens; 15th Amiens to Dover & Ramsgate (Wedgwood (1985), p. 68). These tours were far from holidays and were considered by Pugin as an integral part of his working method.

[38] Eldest son of Sir Richard Sutton, of Lynford Hall, West Tofts, Norfolk, for whom Pugin had worked since 1844 on a series of family commissions. John Sutton, who converted to Catholicism in 1855, brought about the restoration of the chapel at Jesus College, Cambridge on which Pugin had worked from 1846 to 1849. The relationship, both professional and personal, between the Pugin and Sutton families was to persist beyond both Pugin's and (in 1855) Sir

The next morning we left Amiens for Calais. When we were on the boat we met Mr. John Sutton of Norfolk.[38] When we arrived at Dover we went to the Ship Hotel and took a post carriage that evening to Ramsgate. Mr Sutton accompanied us. We had thunder and lightning on the way. My beloved Husband was very poorly indeed. I think it was from over fatigue and the closeness of Paris. I cannot say that this was a very delightful trip as my poor husband was poorly almost the whole week.

In June I had the nurse Mrs. Handford here. My Aunt and Uncle Knill came from Hasting where they had been staying and took a house here on 21st June my birthday. We all went a picnic [sic] near Minster[-in-Thanet]. We enjoyed ourselves very much but on our return I came in my Aunt's carriage which was open and in which I caught a most dreadful cold.

On the 29th I got up early went[?] to 8 o'clock I felt rather ill. Mr Daniel was sent for. My darling little Edmund Peter was born during High Mass about 1/2 past 11 o'clock.[39] I soon recovered my strength but a week afterwards at about 10 o'clock at night, Lucy Margaret's nurse came and told me she must leave that day week, of course I felt it very much as I could do nothing myself. I could not prevent her going also Mary the nursemaid who

---

Richard's deaths. John inherited the baronetcy and was to pay for the completion of the Pugin family chantry chapel at St Augustine's, commissioning the German painter August Martin to paint the altar 'triptych' in the style of the fifteenth century: see A. Jacobs, 'August Martin', *True Principles*, 2, no. 4 (Summer 2002).

[39] 'This day at 1/2 past 11a.m. was born my son Edmund Peter for which thanks be to God for this and all mercies. My dearest Jane doing well.' (Wedgwood, (1985), p. 71). Later known as Peter Paul (1851-1904) this was Pugin's eighth and youngest child. He too became an architect and joined his brothers Edward and Cuthbert to form the firm of Pugin & Pugin. He seems to have changed his name to Peter Paul around 1868, since he signs his letters to Jane 'Edmund Peter' up to this date (ibid., p. 100, n. 10).

had been with us for 8 years left the same week.[40] A week after I heard bad reports of Lucy. The remaining part of the year my dear Husband was constantly away from home preparing for the Great Exhibition during which time he was constantly very much out of health.[41] He was ordered cold splashing baths. One day whilst taking one of these he quite lost himself, his memory quite failed him for about two hours. He had two or three times a strange sensation in his nose, he smelt a strong perfume and almost fainted. In October Anne was confined, [s]he had a little daughter Mildred our first grandchild, her Grand Papa was 40 and myself grandmother 26 years.[42] Anne had swollen breasts and suffered an agony for 5 weeks.[43] She could not nurse her child, it was brought up by hand and now Thank God thrives nicely.

Christmas Day was a very miserable one, for my dear Husband had returned home about three weeks before very ill indeed with a kind of fever.[44] Dr. Grant bishop of Southwark came down to confirm on the [space blank] of

[40] This must have been a difficult summer for Jane. In August she was invited to Alton by Lady Shrewsbury but Pugin wrote to decline the invitation: 'I will not fail to be at Alton on the 11th. Mrs. Pugin is truly sensible of Lady Shrewsbury's great kindness, but I fear it will not be possible for her to leave home, which will be a great disappointment to her, but she has never thoroughly recovered from her confinement & we were obliged to return suddenly from our last journey without completing what we intended & I think it will be safer for me to come alone at this time' (Letter to Lord Shrewsbury, 6th August 1851 in ibid., **69**, p. 115.)

[41] See Spencer-Silver, chapter 3, for a good account of the bustle and temperaments involved in setting up the Mediaeval Court at the Great Exhibition at the Crystal Palace in Hyde Park.

[42] Mildred Powell (1851-1941).

[43] In Birmingham on 30th November 1851, Pugin records a 'vow for Anne's [?] recovery', which Wedgwood speculates may actually have been for Mildred's recovery. Jane's entry confirms what lay behind this prayer.

[44] From 3rd December, Pugin uncharacteristically mentions his health in his own diary (in general, he is more forthcoming about his state of health in his letters to his friends, suppliers and even patrons).

Dec.[45] In the evening of the same day he placed the relic of the H.C. on my husband's head. From that time he said he was better. From this time until Feby he seemed changed much.[46]

[1852]

On the 25th Feby (Ash Wednesday) he said he must go to London consequently at 1/2 past 10 o'clock he left Ramsgate with Edward and having passed 2 dreadful nights and a day in London he was taken to Kensington House by Dr. Tweedie, Messrs Hardman, Myers, Herbert and Edward

---

[45] Pugin notes on 17th December 'The Lord Bishop came' (Wedgwood (1985), p. 72). Dr Thomas Grant was the first Bishop of Southwark in whose diocese Ramsgate lay. Designs survive for floral patterns drawn in the style of the early sixteenth century and inscribed 'Drawn in ink Decr. 18th 1851/ a few minutes after the departure of the Bishop of Dr Grant [sic]/ and receiving a benediction of the H Cross/ carried by his Lordship.' (Ibid., **838**, p. 270) However, by Christmas Day Pugin notes again that he is 'Very unwell[?].' The last entry in his diary is for 30th December 1851. If he started a new volume for 1852, its whereabouts is unknown.

[46] The inscription on a sketch of Ravensburg, Baden-Wurttemberg, suggests Pugin and Jane might have been in Germany in February 1852 ('Ravensburg from Meridian's bird's eye brought to a low horizon by A. W. Pugin in the presence of his dear wife to whom he dedicates this sketch, d. 23rd Feb 1852' : ibid., **972**, p. 287). While such a trip might have been undertaken to improve Pugin's health, Wedgwood speculates that a group of other German subjects made at the same time have apparently been taken from a book (ibid., **956**, p. 284). A poignant poem also survives, written by Pugin to Jane perhaps with another sketch one week before his confinement in Kensington House:

> In this fair head / a Queen you see
> Who ruled over England's lands
> But she is like my little Queen
> Who has my love and lands
> And therefore in this pointed frame
> I set the beauteous head
> Which when I see I think
> Of thee
> Dear Partner of my bed. (Ibid., **98**, p. 121)

on the 27th Feby.[47] I heard nothing of this.[48] I therefore resolved to go to London, which I did and was there told by Mr. Hardman where my dear Husband had been placed. I was not allowed to see him.[49] After repeated entreaties to that effect, he continued there until June when dissatisfaction arose about his being at Kensington.[50] It was therefore resolved he should go to Bethlem [Bedlam] where

[47] According to Ferrey, Pugin was first removed to the Golden Cross in Wellington Street, the Strand 'and put under proper restraint.' When all 'moderate attempts to tranquillize him' failed, he was moved to Kensington House, a private asylum (Ferrey, p. 267). Pugin was at Kensington House from 27th February to 21st June (Margaret Belcher, *A. W. N. Pugin: An Annotated Critical Bibliography* (1987), D456, p. 318).

[48] This is the first example of an apparent conspiracy among Pugin's closest male friends and family members (no doubt well-meaning but a conspiracy nevertheless) to keep Jane away from her husband during the first months of his last illness. Edward, Pugin's eldest son, had just reached his eighteenth birthday that spring.

[49] It seems to have been John Hardman who objected to Jane visiting her husband. See for example HLRO, PUG 3/9/308, letter from Hardman to Jane, (n.d.): 'I think you had better remain quietly in Ramsgate. You can do nothing & it only distresses you & increases expense.' And again on 18th May 1852: 'I shall not enter into any discussion upon the course that has been pursued. I am only sorry that your feelings should have been again wrought up when the end might equally have been gained without it. You do not say but I suppose you have decided to leave your dear husband where he is for the present in accordance with the opinion of the physicians ... Pray try to settle down again as far as you can as it seems quite clear that as long as this violent stage of the mania lasts nothing can be done. The real treatment must commence afterwards.' (HLRO, PUG 3/9/309).

[50] Letters from friends continued to try to reassure but fend off Jane. This from Dr Doyle of St George's on 3rd June 1852: 'I saw him [Pugin] walking in the garden this morning and he walked as well as ever he did. After, a little tired, he sat down and began to draw just as he used to do. The leg is nothing at all and his mind is improving very much. So thank God. It is all a mistake about this delay of letters to you – one thought that the other had written and then the mistake – no one is in fault, that is the truth. Have you any old clothes for him? It is no use buying new clothes for him so please attend to this. The feeling of all parties is this that he will be as well as ever he was in his life. So cheer up and have confidence in God and the prayers of the Blessed Virgin.' (HLRO, PUG 3/9/312).

he was taken on the 21st June <u>my birthday</u>!![51] But during the time between Feby and June Mr. Hardman remained, Mr & Mrs Powell, Edward and all the young men from the studio – Hendren, Hurley, Hill, Myer so that the church was then left almost without servers.[52] Anne played until the middle of July and the boys managed to sing pretty well but when Anne left a young man of the name of Plastrer[?] (now a lay brother) played dreadfully so badly that I said there had better be no music.

[51] Jane signed the application for Pugin's admission on 17th June and so was an active party to the decision. Bedlam, now the Imperial War Museum, was chiefly a pauper asylum, at this date harbouring the criminally insane as well the mentally ill, although the admission form distinguishes those whose friends stood security. In Pugin's case, John and Stuart Knill put up a bond of £100 (see Belcher (1987), D456, p. 317). Reports in the *Builder* in July and *The Times* suggested that the straightened circumstances of the architect's family played a part in this transfer, presumably misunderstanding the distinction made by the admission form and therefore inferring a lack of means. There were rumours of a public subscription for the family, to which Lord John Russell volunteered a donation of £10. All this brought a brusque rebuttal from eighteen-year-old Edward, who wrote, according to Ferrey, 'I trust I may be able to carry out my father's professional engagements; and with the continued assistance of his family and friends, to maintain the family until such time as it may please God to restore him to us' (Ferrey, p. 270). A draft letter in an unknown hand to the editor of the *Morning Post* is also to be found in HLRO, PUG 3/9/314, which implies that the treatment available at Bedlam was in fact preferable to that at a private asylum. Nor would the general public have been aware of other possibly contributory factors in the decision to move Pugin to Bedlam. St George's Cathedral could be seen from its windows and the redoubtable George Myers, Pugin's builder, lived in nearby Laurie Terrace. In May 1852 Myers had won the contract for alterations to be made at Bedlam instructed by the newly appointed Physician Superintendent of the hospital, the enlightened Dr William Charles Hood (Spencer-Silver, p. 75). According to Edward Pugin a decade later, the reason for the decision to place his father in Bedlam was 'that a professional man, personally known to my father's friends, had just left that institution, perfectly restored; and all agreed that he would there receive the best professional treatment and be at the same time under the constant care of his old friend, Dr Doyle of St. George's.' (Letter written to *Blackwood's Edinburgh Magazine* in February 1862 (see Belcher, D456, p. 317).

[52] This incomplete sentence implies that all those named left Ramsgate and went to work at Hardman's in Birmingham. Of those mentioned, Hardman Powell writes '[Pugin] built a Cartoon Room in his Garden, covered its walls

On July 21st I went to Bethlem with Revd. J. M. Glenie [*sic*] to see my husband.[53] It was at first refused but at last I was allowed to see him, I was indeed shocked, he did not know me, he looked half the size he was, his hair was shaved off, in fact he was so much altered that if he had been with others I would not have known him. He looked certainly 70.[54] The sensation I felt on seeing him I cannot describe, but I was very quiet. I kissed him several times but I neither spoke or cried, they only allowed me to remain with him 3 minutes. Mr Glenie then remained with him a little, he drew him a rough sketch of a Church. We came away from the place fully determined to recover him for it was quite evident he was sinking, his voice was quite altered.

Mr. Glenie then spoke to me about Dr. Dickson of Bolton Street, Piccadilly. He had already spoken to him about my dear Husband & he said he was curable if he could be placed under his care, but how was this to be done? I knew not. I would have taken him myself but this was not safe. Mr. Glenie then like a real Christian offered to take a house and take charge of him. I of course was delighted at the idea but then there were others to consult because it was a very serious undertaking. Mr. Glenie and myself went to meet my Uncle Mr. John Knill and Mr. Hardman at Shot Lodge Blackheath (my Uncle's house). He told them what he proposed doing, they both thought it a

with fine carvings and casts, and got Hardman to send youths who shewed marked gifts for Art, from the works at Birmingham to be trained by himself. Frederick Hill, Edwin Hendren, John Early, (all fortunately having good voices) formed a strong addition to the choir and later on at Pugin's death they carried on the work, as far as was possible in his spirit' (Wedgwood (1988), p. 184).

[53] The Rev. John Melville Glennie (1816-78) had been received into the Catholic Church at Oscott in 1845. He was ordained in 1851, worked at Southwark, and was a good friend of the Pugins.

[54] The implication is that Jane has not been allowed to see her husband since his committal to Kensington House in February. It would seem that it was these three months that accounted for his most serious decline.

mad scheme but said little. Mr. Glenie left and then next morning Mr. Hardman tried to dissuade me from it, said we could not rely on Dr. Dickson's treatment and a great deal more. We afterwards called on Dr. Dixon [*sic*], he referred me to Dr. Fergusson to consult him about the chloroform. He assured us there could be no danger but he referred us to Dr. Snow. After this we met at the House of Lords, Hardman, Herbert, Mr. Glenie, Powell, my Uncle Mr. John Knill & myself. They said "Now Mrs. Pugin, it is for you to decide if he is to be removed or not, we cannot take responsibility." So I immediately said "I find everything else has been tried, instead of getting better he is much worse. I have seen him, he looks 70. I should not have known him he is so altered. If he remains in Bethlem I am quite sure he will die so this is the only chance left. I will take the responsibility upon myself.["][55] After this Herbert quite agreed with, me so it was decided we should rather take a house[56] & that he should be removed there. Accordingly the Committee were spoken to & he was to be removed in a fortnight. I returned to Ramsgate, packed up all I wanted, prepared a costume for myself consisting of a black petticoat & coloured jacket, white apron and plain cap with curls, it quite altered me.

On 29th July I went to London with Emma Newy[?] my

---

[55] This is consistent with Edward's letter to *Blackwood's Edinburgh Magazine* (Belcher, D456, p. 317) in which he writes 'my father's removal [from Bedlam] was solely at the instance of his wife, who, in conjunction with the Rev. Mr. Glennie, acted in opposition to the wishes of his other friends (who were satisfied with his treatment and progress whilst at Bethlehem).' It is hard to disagree with Jane's decision to move Pugin as we read her descriptions of his relative physical and mental conditions in Bedlam compared with his apparent rally at Hammersmith Grove, but in the light of his subsequent death, such public statements by her stepson of her lone responsibility for the change in treatment must have been distressing.

[56] 'decided', i.e., that the family should pay for a house rather than Mr Glennie.

cook. We drove to 16 Grove Hammersmith [*sic*]. The family by name Hawkins were still there but removed that evening. We had enough to do to get the house to rights for my dear Husband the next day as of course all breakable things had to be stowed away. The next day the 30th July my dearly beloved husband arrived at the Grove about 1/2 past 5. I cannot describe my feelings when I saw him so altered get out of the cab. He seemed delighted coming as he thought on a visit to Mr. Glenie, he asked immediately for his tea. He took ten cups of tea, a whole 1/2 quartern loaf & 3 chops. This of course was a very bad sign for a person in health would not have so ravenous an appetite. Dr. Dixon and Dr. Snow arrived in the evening to give the Chloroform, how I dreaded it! Not knowing the effect it would have, I felt too much to be present so I prayed most fervently during the time. What a relief to me when they told me it was all right, I then went to look at him. Well, he was fast asleep, quite calm and comfortable. How old and changed he looked but still the thought of his again being in the same house & that I should have a chance of waiting on him once more made me feel happier than I had done since he left home. I did not think it right to let him see me that evening. The next morning I went to wait upon him. He called me Mary Amherst but I said I was Mrs Kight[?] the housekeeper.[57] Dr Dixon continued his treatment of chloroform for 3 days. He then had to go to Ireland for a

---

[57] Mary Amherst (1824-60) was sister to another friend, Francis Kerril Amherst, who became Bishop of Northampton. After Pugin's second wife Louisa's sudden death in August 1844, Pugin wanted very much to marry Mary and had proposed in November of the same year ('November 10 - ... sent proposal to Mrs. Amherst' – Wedgwood (1985), p. 56 and n. 47). It seems her parents did not think him worthy of their daughter and in May 1846, Mary became a nun. Her mother, Mrs Amherst, had paid for the erection of the Catholic church of St Augustine, Kenilworth, designed by Pugin and completed in 1841 (ibid., p. 86, n. 41).

week. During that time poor Augustus was often very violent as we discontinued use of the chloroform. Thank God I pacified him several times. One night in particular about 1 o'clock I heard a terrible noise. I went down and asked Mr Glenie if I could be of any use. He said he thought not but he would see, he then asked the 2 keepers if I could be of any use, "Can Mrs Pugin be of any use." Poor Augustus said, "Yes tell her she can be of great use of [sic] me." So of course immediately I heard and went in. He was there being held down by 2 Keepers with a counterpane over him calling out most awfully. I asked him what was the matter, what could I do for him. He said, "These men are holding me down, let me go." So I said "If I let you go, will you be quiet," so he said "Yes, I will." So I took the counterpane off & I laid my head on his pillow. He went to sleep for two hours as quiet as possible. I felt so happy that I had been in some small degree the means of giving him a little ease and quiet.

[30th July scored out]

3rd August Dr Dicks [sic] left for Ireland. In his absence Dr [-?-] Winslow[?] from whom we had had the first keeper sent for him [the keeper] at a few hours notice. This was very bad as he [Winslow] had sent him to us without any conditions. I therefore had to get two common men for the morning. In my absence he had a very violent paroxism [sic] and on my return I found they had tied him in an armchair. He was screaming out awfully, calling on Mary Amherst and Mrs W[-?-]. It was then near his dinnertime. I cut up some meat and took it in. I asked him if he would have his dinner, he said "yes," then [I] fed him. I told Mr Glenie that I was quite sure it would be better for him to be unfastened. Consequently they untied him. He became perfectly calm & quiet and sat drawing for more than an hour.

5th & 6th August I procured 2 Keepers. One he called

Adam, a great tall strong unpleasant looking man. He had been a soldier. The other he called Alladin, brother-in-law to the other. I did not like either of them, they could not bear me to be with him. They said I made him worse but they knew the contrary but I was always watching and listening. This they did not like at all so several times when I was away they spoke to Mr Glenie saying they wished he would use his influence with me to prevent me being with him. I also heard that Adam had said that when we went to Ramsgate he would ask me to set up a room for himself and my beloved Husband. This looked as though he wished to install himself with us, so altogether I did not like them at all. Dr Dickson also said he felt as if he had not fair play so of course this confirmed me in my opinion. I sent off a telegraphic message to Mayman our carpenter in Ramsgate to come up by the next train. Fearing the Keeper might guess what I intended to do I met him at 8 in the evening and told him to go to sleep at the inn and come up in the morning. In the morning he came, it was 27th. When Mayman came into the room my beloved Husband knew him immediately and called him by his name. I then called each of the other men, paid them their wages also a week in advance. I made them a present of a week too, so that they might go off in good humour. Mayman seemed to understand his place very well. I enquired for another man as two were necessary. A nice old man applied, directly my beloved Husband saw him, he called him in. He called him Hogarth, believing he was the great painter, from that time we all called him Hogarth (Mr Carter). He came on the 28th. He certainly appeared more happy. By degrees I left off my costume and on the 29th I think it was I went out to walk with him. As we were crossing the field he stopped suddenly and said, "Jane, are you not my wife." I said, "Yes I am dearest." ["]Oh["], he said, ["]how kind you are to come and take care of me. I will never leave you again. Have we not got a house at Ramsgate, why do we not go there? Do let us go back.["] I said we should as soon as he was well, he was almost quite himself, how happy I thought myself to see him again so like himself. I cried for joy and returned home. You may imagine how happy I felt, I saw he must certainly be better to remember all he did and that he really knew who I was, this was a great blessing. It was really edifying to hear him. When it was 12 o'clock or about 6 he used almost always to say the Angelus, or a part of it, and sometimes he used to ask for his Office Book, and say a little of that. This little instance shews that these little acts of devotion & piety must have been deeply rooted in his soul. The evening of the day on which he first recognised me was the first time I entirely left off my curls, cap & jacket.

After this he frequently had paroxysms but on the Sunday I have just spoken of, he said "as you are my wife, why do you not sleep with me." I said that he had been ill and that the doctors would not allow it as he did not sleep and that my health would be ruined. I said this because I knew the idea of hurting me would have more effect on him. He promised that if I would, he would sleep all night. Accordingly, as night came on I thought he would not remember my promise, but I was surprised to hear him say "Now Jane dear remember your promise." At this moment I felt a little nervous but I was his wife, I had devoted myself to him & I felt happy in running some risk for love of him. We went to bed and much to my surprise he fell asleep almost immediately saying how happy he felt.

The next morning he was better and continued to improve daily until the 3rd. He went that day to Mr Glenie's, looked at the Chapel and the House and the Church then building. He returned home to me and told me how the other architect had copied all his designs. I comforted him as well as I could. He then began to [blank] all the furniture in the room just like he usually did [-?-] all the modern furniture in the bedroom, laughed heartily, a thing he had not done for so long, I felt alive with joy, felt almost sure he would recover. Received that mor[ning] £50 from Hardman with a letter from him in which he begs I should not be extravagant. This I felt fearfully as I certainly was not so, of course I spared nothing on my beloved Husband, I felt I would sooner beg than that he should not have every comfort he required. Hardman had also sent a message by Edward previously to the effect that he/Hardman thought I had better return to Ramsgate for fear I should <u>forget</u> how to take care of the house and my children. I told Edward to tell Mr Hardman that for the future I begged he would choose another messenger and that he was to tell Hardman that my husband was my first care, my best love and that to save him if it was necessary my house and all should go to rack and ruin sooner than my husband should be neglected in the slightest degree. Whether Edward gave my message to Hardman I know not but he left me in peace for a time. This happened about the 3rd.

About the 6th he was not quite so well, the weather became damp & I noticed he dragged one leg slightly. I spoke to Dr Dixon about it on the 10th. Dr D agreed we should return to Ramsgate. It was Friday. I packed up everything and sent the children and 3 servants home by the 11 train on Saturday am.[58] I intended leaving at the same time but I asked the station master to keep a carriage for my Husband by the 3 train. He said, "What is the matter with him." I said he was not quite right. He said, "What do you mean, is he mad, if so I cannot keep a carriage for him." I

---

[58] This is the only suggestion that Jane was joined in Hammersmith by her children.

was so hurt & disgusted and fearing there might be some difficulty when dear Margaret arrived at the station, I saw the children off and returned in a cab to Hammersmith hoping to be in time before he started. Fortunately I saw his carriage at the door. We provided a large packet of ham sandwiches and started. At first he appeared very pleased but as we came near the station he saw so many people he became quite alarmed and said he would not go to Ramsgate, that he would rather return to Hammersmith. I did not know what to do as it was near the time for the train starting and I had given up the key to the house so Mayman & Hogarth gave him a little chloroform, just sufficient to stupify him. In this state he was assisted out of the carriage but the noise of the people and dreadful rush to obtain seats as it was Saturday afternoon made me fear I should not be able to find a carriage with 4 places. I had asked my Uncle Mr John Knill & Stuart to meet me at the station & secure a carriage. I saw them but they had [not] done so. I was nearly distracted as Augustus was coming to himself and I feared he might make a noise and attract attention. My Uncle unkindly told me I looked more like a mad thing than anything else. I told [him] I thought under [the] circumstances I had enough to make me so, but I must say I felt very much hurt at this remark. Being driven almost to despair I said to the station master "For God's Sake get me a carriage." My manner of course was very earnest. He said "In one moment." At that instant a carriage was brought up in which I placed Augustus, Mayman & Hogarth, also a gentleman who knew him once at Oscott but I do not remember his name.[59] The train soon started and dear Augustus appeared much pleased. By degrees he eat [*sic*] the

---

[59] St Mary's College, Oscott – see note 7.

sandwiches, they were finished by the time we reached Canterbury. He then became very tired & said he would much rather have gone down by water but he remained quiet and as soon as we arrived at Ramsgate we took a fly and drove home where everything was ready & comfortable. He was delighted with the house, the books & pictures, he asked where his sketches were.[60] I told him I had sent them down to Birmingham to be taken care of at which he seemed satisfied. He would not go to bed but remained up all night explaining all the prints & pictures to Hogarth at which I was very sorry as I knew not was [*sic*] the best thing for him. On Sunday he appeared better and drew a little. Amongst other things he gathered a rose which was growing near the Library window, drew it and wrote upon it "Drawn in the presence of my dear wife Jane the XII Sept 1852" which I now preserve with great care. He wished to assist at Mass but he afterwards said he would not, he would not [*sic*] go to bed again. That night I think Hardman sat up.

Monday 13th [September 1852] He appeared much better, so much so that he & I had a walk near the Cliff with one [every?] one near at first. I did not feel at all fearful but when I had gone half way I thought it would be more prudent to turn up near a walk in Mr Warr's field from which place we had a very good view of the house. He turned round to me & said, "Jane my dear it is a beautiful place is it not? It is all yours, my dear wife, what a good wife you have been to me." He then cried, kissed me and said, "How can I thank you for all you have done for me, I shall never leave you again, but you shall take care of me." He appeared quite himself but his mind was quite weak. I then felt I would live for him, I could never do enough for him.

---

[60] Pugin kept the topographical sketches made on his study tours in bound volumes and they were an important source of inspiration and reference for his work.

We walked up to St Lawrence & came down the narrow lane & coming up through Spencer Square I heard a band playing music fell [*sic*] like a dead weight upon my heart. I felt dreadfully miserable.

We return[ed] home and he changed his things, he was shaved, I washed his face. He said I was a dear good wife and that he would do all I asked him to do. I then begged him to go to bed early that night, he said he would. We went down to the Library, he lay upon the sofa. I was sitting by him and Daniel our doctor came in. Augustus was so glad to see him, knew him perfectly and talked sensibly but strayed once or twice. He [Daniel] left and we sat in the garden on the iron seat.[61] He slept for a short time until teatime, which he enjoyed very much. He went to bed at 8 o'clock. I forgot to say that about 2 o'clock he & I went into the Church. He was delighted with everything he saw, said it was beautiful. He had his Office Book from which he repeated Primer, he knelt before the image of Our Lady saying a little prayer. We left the Church & sat in the garden.

About 11 o'clock he woke me by getting out of bed. I jumped up to see what was the matter, he had his eyes fixed. I called out his name, he only said "Jane I am going." Dr Beamish was sent for as being the nearest & then Daniel. They ordered a warm bath and then leeches on his temples. I implored of them not to put them on but they said he would die if they did not, what could I do. If they had not applied them & he had died it would have been my misery for life. I telegraphed to Dr Dixon, to my Uncle, Edward & Mr Hardman. The next morning Thursday Augustus looked very ill. He was in a state of stupor, he never spoke again. Dr Dix arrived at 3, he gave him brandy & water & said the Doctors ought not to have put on the leeches. It was a

---

[61] Perhaps the iron seat shown in Pugin's 1849 watercolour of *A True Prospect of St. Augustine's*: see Fig. 4.

fearful time. He blamed me for allowing them to be put them [*sic*] on, I had done my best but I was no doctor and the doctors were all against me. Father Costagan came and anointed my beloved Husband and at 10 minutes to 5 he died!!

I cannot describe my feelings. My lonely desolate condition. My Uncle John Knill came. I begged of him in my agony to be kind to me. I felt left to everyone's mercy. None but those who have passed through the same scenes – "that first dark day of nothingness!" [as page heading] can have the faintest idea of what I mean.

Many came down to the funeral, it is [*sic*] a solemn sight when the coffin was carried at [*sic*] moonlight through the garden and as it was being carried through the garden the front bell rang. It sounded so melancholy I can hear it now. We then had Matins. The next morning Dr Grant sang high Mass and the coffin was lowered into the vault.[62] I felt as if I could have gone in after it. I can well remember my poor children looking on unconscious of their loss.[63] Poor children, God alone knows who will take care of them.

After all was over, the will was opened. It was found to be only a small piece of paper in which he leaves everything to me for me to dispose of as I thought best for the children signed by himself and John Powell and Edward had signed his name on the envelope which of course was of no service.[64] In fact it was better as it was for it would have caused great discontent amongst the children. I knew

[62] Dr Grant took as the text for his funeral sermon *Ecclesiasticus*, 15:6, 'Rich men in virtue, studying beautifulness: living at peace in their houses', an appropriate and graceful tribute to both the man and the house he built for himself.

[63] Edmund (later known as Peter Paul) was just a year old, Margaret nearly three. Jane is clearly writing after the event, although the following passage suggests it was not long after.

[64] The lack of adequate witnesses meant that Pugin effectively died intestate.

nothing of what was in the paper, we seldom spoke upon the subject, but when did so once or twice, I begged him to leave to each child what they were to have, for if I survived him, no matter what I did I should be considered unjust being their stepmother. So as things were the law of gavelkind existing, the house and land was [*sic*] divided equally between the 3 boys and the money, I having one third the remainder was divided equally between all the children.[65] In consequence of this arrangement everything we possessed had to be turned into money, so with the exception of a few books and pictures, everything was sold at Sotheby & Wilkinson's by Waterloo Bridge. They only fetched £2,000 although this was fearful for the library alone cost £3,000 without the pictures. Amongst the pictures we had two fine Albert Durers for which Augustus had given for repairing, framing & c. £500. John Hardman of Birmingham bought them for £52 the pr. !!!! My cousin Stuart Knill bought a fine map of Bruges which Lord Shrewsbury had given to Augustus surmounted with the Shrewsbury arms for 4'/ !!! The others went in proportion so the years poor Augustus had spent in collecting things were completely thrown away. If he had thought everything would be sold by the summer he would I am sure have broken his heart. Poor Augustus![66]

Edward had already gone down to Birmingham, it was now for us to decide where we should live. Hardman

---

[65] When Jane was granted administration of his property in December 1852, the estate was valued at £10,000 (Belcher, D456, p. 317 and p. 319).

[66] The sale of books was held in January 1853 and lasted three days. It raised £1083 2s. 6d. Pugin's carvings and *objets d'art* were sold on 12th February 1853 and made £429 10s. 6d. His paintings, drawings and engravings went under the hammer on 7th April raising £598 11s. 6d. This passage therefore dates Jane's latter entries at least as having been written more than six months after Pugin's death. See D. J. Watkin (editor), *Sales Catalogues of Eminent Persons* (Mansell & Sotheby, Park-Bernet Publications, 1972) for the full sale list.

strongly advised me to live with my 2 children near my Uncle at Blackheath. My Uncle was equally energetic in urging me to live near Hardman on account of what he would do for us. To Hardman I said that if my Uncle intended to give me anything, he would do so without my going to live near him, that I could not do such a thing with such a notion, it was really <u>too mean</u>. To my Uncle I said I certainly intended going down to Birmingham not for what Hardman would do for me but as I was left Mother of a family young as I was I was competent to make a home for the children because if there was no home, the children would be scattered, never again to be united. In fact the family as a family would be broken up. Hardman strongly opposed me, may God forgive me if I misjudge him but I feel sure he had his own selfish notions for wishing such a thing thinking he would have more influence over Edward and easily marry him to one of his daughters.

Indeed I can pretty justly say that this was the case because one day before we left Ramsgate, I went into the Church. I heard voices I could not tell from where they came. At last I found there was someone in the South porch. Thinking it might be someone who ought not to be there, I listened for a moment and heard old Mrs Powell John Powell's mother say "she says she is quite sure John Hardman wishes Edward to marry one of his daughters and she says she would not like it at all." In answer John Powell said "and a very good thing it would be if he did so." A cold shudder ran through me, I then saw how desolate I was, the one John Powell who I thought quite on our side was against me. From that moment my mind was made up to go to Birmingham. I desired Edward to take a house in Birmingham for me.

[In a later version of her hand:]

Oh! the Power of pure Simplicity!

"Were a Star quenched on high
For ages would its light
Still travelling downwards from the Sky
Shine on our mortal sight
So when a great man dies
For years beyond our ken
The light he leaves around him lies
Upon the paths of men."[67]

"Go set thy foot on winged heath [?]
Or unto Honour's Tower's aspire
Give me but my Freedom & my Health
The Sum of my Desire!"

Ramsgate '76

[Here the journal ends. The back end paper has barely legible jottings against dates relating to the events recorded in the journal for August and September 1852.]

---

[67] Henry Wadsworth Longfellow, *Charles Sumner*, stanzas 8 & 9, *The Poetical Works of Longfellow* (1975 edition, Routledge & Co.), p. 324. The quotation is touching evidence of Jane's continuing devotion to her husband's memory more than twenty years after his death.

BIBLIOGRAPHY

♦♦♦

Primary Sources

A photocopy and microfilm of Jane Pugin's journal may be found in the House of Lords Record Office (HLRO) as PUG 3/15 or DIAZO 387 respectively. The copyright for the text of the journal remains with its private owner and permission to reproduce any portion of its text must be sought from the HLRO.

The chief deposits of Pugin papers are to be found at the HLRO, the Victoria and Albert Museum and the Library of the Royal Institute of British Architects (RIBA) although a significant minority remain in private ownership. At the time of publication, volumes 1 and 2 of Margaret Belcher's edition of *The Collected Letters of A. W. N. Pugin* have been published, covering the years 1830-42 (Oxford University Press, Oxford, 2001) and 1843-5 (2003). Jane and Pugin's married years must therefore await the future volumes, which will no doubt shed more light on their relationship.

Secondary Sources

Atterbury, Paul (editor), *A. W. N. Pugin: Master of the Gothic Revival* (Yale University Press, New Haven and London, 1995).

Atterbury, Paul and Wainwright, Clive, (editors), *Pugin: A Gothic Passion* (Yale University Press, New Haven and London, 1994).

Belcher, Margaret, *A. W. N. Pugin: An Annotated Critical Bibliography* (Mansell, London, 1987).

Blaker, Catriona, *Edward Pugin and Kent*, (Pugin Society, Ramsgate, 2003).

Bogan, Bernard, *The Great Link: A History of St. George's, Southwark* (Burns and Oates, London, 1948).

Ferrey, Benjamin, *Recollections of A. W. N. Pugin and his Father Augustus Pugin* (Edward Stanford, London, 1861). See also 1978 reprint, with an introduction and index by Clive and Jane Wainwright, published by the Scolar Press, London.

Egan, Michael , 'Mrs Jane Pugin and some London Relations', *True Principles*, 2 no. 4 (Summer 2002), pp. 22-4.

Spencer-Silver, Patricia , *Pugin's Builder: The Life and Works of George Myers* (University of Hull Press, Hull, 1993).

Trappes-Lomax, Michael, *Pugin: A Medieval Victorian* (Sheen & Ward, London, 1932).

Wedgwood, Alexandra, *The Pugin Family, Catalogues of the Drawings Collection of the Royal Institute of British Architects* (Gregg International, Farnborough, 1977).

Wedgwood, Alexandra, *A. W. N. Pugin and the Pugin Family, Catalogues of the Architectural Drawings at the Victoria and Albert Museum* (Victoria and Albert Museum, London, 1985).

Wedgwood, Alexandra, 'Pugin in his Home: A Memoir by J. H. Powell', *Architectural History*, 31 (1988), pp. 171-201.

Fig. 14
Perspective of The Grange from the south-east – proof of an etching by
A. W. N. Pugin, *c*.1849. The children playing in the garden makes this
unequivocally a view of the family house. Unlike the bird's eye view watercolour painted around the same time (Fig. 4) The Grange is here shown as
built without breaks in the masonry line of this garden elevation.
(*Victoria & Albert Museum Drawings Collection*)

THE GRANGE
&
THE LANDMARK TRUST

♦ ♦ ♦

Founded in 1965, the Landmark Trust is a charity that rescues historic buildings that might not otherwise survive and gives them a new future by offering them for holidays. Today, there are almost 200 Landmark buildings across Great Britain in which anyone can stay.

Once a building has been restored, the income generated is put towards its future upkeep and gives it a sustainable future. However, Landmark must raise the money for the initial restoration.

The Grange in Ramsgate is the house that Augustus Pugin designed and built to live in with his family. The last of Pugin's children, Cuthbert, lived there until his death in 1928. The house then became a school, before passing into private ownership in 1990. It came on the market again in 1997 in a state of advancing decay and with talk of planning permission to turn it into flats, despite its Grade I listed status.

With the help of a grant from the Heritage Lottery Fund, Landmark was able to step in and purchase The Grange to prevent this from happening. The last six years have been spent researching all aspects of the building and raising the significant sums required for its restoration.

The current volume arose out of research done by Landmark on The Grange, which plays almost as significant a role in its pages as do Augustus and Jane Pugin. Restoration of The Grange will begin in 2004. Landmark is grateful for generous donations from the Heritage Lottery Fund, English Heritage and many private donors to enable the restoration of this seminal building and continues to welcome all donations.

All royalties from the sale of this volume will go towards Landmark's fund for the restoration of The Grange.

To make a donation to Landmark's work at The Grange or to find out how to stay there for a holiday, please contact:

The Landmark Trust
Shottesbrooke
Maidenhead
SL6 3SW

01628 825920

www.landmarktrust.co.uk

INDEX

◆ ◆ ◆

Italics indicate illustrations.